HB Playwrights Short Play Festival 2000

THE FUNERAL PLAYS

HB Playwrights Foundation, founded in 1965 by Herbert Berghof and Uta Hagen, has provided an artistic home to more than 130 playwrights since it first opened its doors. Thirty-seven years, 270 full productions and countless staged readings later, it still makes available a safe and nurturing environment where theater artists come to work, free of the pressures of commercial theater. At the HB Playwrights Theatre, admission is free and critics are not invited so, playwrights, assisted by the actors, directors, designers, and other theater artists who volunteer their time, are free to take risks solely for the sake of their art. The Annual HB Short Play Series is one of the great success stories born of the artistic spirit first put into motion by Herbert and Uta so many years ago.

Robert Callely, Managing Director, HB Playwrights Theatre

OTHER BOOKS IN THE SERIES

HB Playwrights Short Play Festival 1997: The Motel Plays

HB Playwrights Short Play Festival 1998: The Museum Plays

HB Playwrights Short Play Festival 1999: The Airport Plays

HB Playwrights
Short Play Festival 2000

THE FUNERAL PLAYS

Edited by William Carden

CONTEMPORARY PLAYWRIGHTS SERIES

A Smith and Kraus Book

A Smith and Kraus Book
Published by Smith and Kraus, Inc.
177 Lyme Road, Hanover, NH 03755
www.SmithKraus.com

Manufactured in the United States of America

Cover and Text Design by Julia Hill Gignoux, Freedom Hill Design
Cover Illustration by Lisa Goldfinger

First Edition: December 2002
10 9 8 7 6 5 4 3 2 1

Contemporary Playwrights Series ISSN 1067-9510
ISBN 1-57525-286-4

CONTENTS

INTRODUCTION

The Funeral Plays is the fourth collection of short plays written for a single location by members of the Playwrights Unit at the HB Playwrights Foundation and Theatre. The story of how the unit got started and along with it this annual festival of short plays is told in the introduction to the first volume in this series, *The Motel Plays.* Now it was four years later. We had increased the number of participating writers and Pamela Berlin had joined as us the director of the Playwrights Unit. Under her guidance, since we now had more writers contributing plays, everyone worked to keep the plays as close to the ten-minute length as possible. Pushing the writers to honor the ten-minute form yielded plays that became more potent and resonant because every moment was made to count. As one of the playwrights, Donna de Matteo said, "It forced me to lift my two babbling characters from the pool of dialogue they seemed to be drowning in and propel them into immediate action." As a result the plays in this volume are admirably lean and compact. They demonstrate how in the hands of a skilled writer, a lot can happen in a very short time.

These plays were presented long before the now popular television series *Six Feet Under* started making the funeral home a more familiar place. At the time, we felt that it was a an adventurous choice for a location and were eager to see where the writers would go with it. As in the past, that turned out to be in many directions. Inevitably, the body in the coffin plays an important role in many of the plays. In four of them that person actually comes to life. Embalming is featured in some, a few deal with eulogies that need to be spoken to honor the deceased and others focus on the unexpected encounters that occur between people brought together by the death of someone they knew. What is most surprising is how much humor there turns out to be in a place we typically associate with solemnity. Almost all of the plays have it in one form or another, from the farcical to the deeply ironic. In that way I think the spectrum of these plays reflects the myriad responses humans have to confronting the common factor that we all share, that none of us will be here forever.

When we produced the plays we presented all them in two evenings of eight plays each that alternated for the course of the run. The single set that adjusted to accommodate the requirements of each play was designed by Vicki Davis and the lighting design that easily moved from the real to the imaginary was by Rene Molina. All the actors, directors, and designers who work at the HB Playwrights Foundation and Theatre donate their time and without their generous commitment to developing new work none of these plays would have been brought to life.

William Carden
Artistic Director

AFTERTHOUGHT

by Neena Beber

To Margarita Ebanks, much in my life;
actor and musician Max Cantor, whom I miss in my life;
and Randolph Walker, whom I never had the chance to know.

ORIGINAL PRODUCTION

Afterthought was directed by Linsay Firman with the following cast:

James	Hamish Linklater
Walter	Joseph Jamrog
Lauren	Beth Bartley
Kyle	Evan Robertson
Writer	Trevor A. Williams

PLAYWRIGHT'S BIOGRAPHY

Neena Beber's plays include *The Dew Point, Hard Feelings, A Common Vision, Tomorrowland, The Brief But Exemplary Life of the Living Goddess,* and *Failure to Thrive.* Theaters that have premiered her work include The Magic Theatre, New Georges, The Women's Project, Theatre J (Washington, D.C.), Padua Hills Playwrights Festival, Workhouse, Urban Empire, The Ivy Theatre (L.A.), En Garde Arts, Echo's Ojai Theatre Festival, and Gloucester Stage. *Jump Slash Cut* received the L. Arnold Weissberger Award in 2001. *Misreadings,* a ten-minute play commissioned and produced by Actors Theatre of Louisville's Humana Festival, is included in *The Best American Short Plays 1996–1997* (Applause). An evening of her short pieces, *Acts of Desire,* premiered at Watermark Theatre. The short film *Bad Dates* (Touchstone) was based on her one-act *Food,* published in *Facing Forward* (Broadway Play Publishing). She has received an A.S.K. Exchange to The Royal Court Theater, an Amblin Commission from Playwrights Horizons, an Otterbein Commission, a MacDowell Colony Fellowship, and a Distinguished Alumni Award from NYU's Tisch School of the Arts, where she was a Paulette Goddard Fellow for her MFA, BA, Harvard University. She is a member of New Dramatists, The New York Playwrights Lab, The Women's Project, and, with gratitude, the HB Playwrights Foundation.

AFTERTHOUGHT

A stage dressed as a funeral parlor. A young couple, James and Lauren, stand beside a coffin.

JAMES: What I've been trying to say, is . . . is . . . not only do I love you, but —

(Walter, looking like a waiter, approaches and serves the couple. He could be putting on an accent, a bit thickly.)

WALTER: A nice merlot for the lovely lady; Scotch with a twist for the gentleman.

LAUREN: Thank you.

(Walter stays there, watching.)

WALTER: Will there be anything else, then?

JAMES: Everything is quite all right, thanks.

WALTER: Beautiful day, is it not?

LAUREN: It is; it's a beautiful day.

JAMES: Now we'd like to seize the day on our own, if you don't mind.

WALTER: Very good, Sir. Good luck, Sir. The perfect time and place, if I may say.

(Walter turns back and gives James a thumbs-up sign.)

LAUREN: Does he seem a little strange to you?

JAMES: What's strange, Claire —

(As Walter goes off, he backs into a coffin and knocks down a wreath. James rolls his eyes.)

JAMES: What's strange, Claire, is that you think about this moment, you plan it, you play it again and again in your dead . . . head . . . but although it may never really possible to know another soul, to know their hopes and dreams and sorrows, after six weeks together I know that you're the one I want to — *(James gets down on one knee. The coffin is in the way.)* Ow.

(Kyle stands; comes forward from the audience.)

KYLE: Let's keep going.

JAMES: *(Standing, annoyed.)* Ow ow ow ow ow!

KYLE: I may need to reblock a bit later.

JAMES: A "bit"?

KYLE: Let's just stumble through, please. From "what's strange . . ."

JAMES: *(Deep breath.)* What's . . . strange . . . shit.

(Kyle comes onto the stage.)

KYLE: You're doing beautifully.

JAMES: This feels all wrong, Kyle.

KYLE: Make that work for you, James. You want her, you're afraid, she might say no, she might say yes, you're taking that leap . . . you might not want to play the fear so hard, but I like what's coming through.

JAMES: What's coming through is, is the ridiculousness of our situation.

KYLE: What's the problem?

JAMES: I'm — this is a coffin.

KYLE: It's all about the focus. You stay focused, we stay focused on you. Focus, James.

(James shakes his head but gives it a go.)

JAMES: What's strange, Claire, is that you think about this moment . . . you . . .

(James stops, frustrated, trying to block out the scenery.)

KYLE: Use it, James. Use the obstacle.

JAMES: These conditions, these conditions are bogus, Kyle. I cannot perform under these conditions.

KYLE: Where is your imagination? Where is your ability to transform? Can a funeral wreath not be a lovely courtyard garden? Can a coffin not be an espresso bar? Lauren, you don't have a problem with the set, do you?

LAUREN: Maybe if we could just get rid of the coffin?

(Walter starts to move it.)

KYLE: Don't touch! Do you realize how lucky we are to have this slot to do our play AT ALL? Don't worry about the set. That is my job. That is not your job. Worry about the words, James.

JAMES: *(Giving it a go.)* What's strange, Claire, is that you think about this moment, you plan it, you play it again and again in your . . . head . . . *(Getting down on one knee.)* . . . but although it may never really be possible to know another soul, to know their hopes and dreams and sorrows, after six weeks together I know that you're the one I want to — Claire, death — dear — will you bury me? Marry me?

LAUREN: Yes, I . . . line . . .

KYLE: Will.

LAUREN: Sorry. Right. Yes, I — *(About to get back in the moment, but can't.)* I am very sensitive to place. When I was in South Carolina to shoot the Nicorette thing last year I developed a Southern accent, and when I'm in a bar I drink, a little too much, even though I don't drink, and I am sensitive to place and I don't want to think about death, thank you.

KYLE: This happens when one leaves the safety of the rehearsal room for the real stage. This is nerves, that's all, normal nerves.

JAMES: We are not nervous, we are distracted. We are surrounded by, by the accoutrements of death and that is rather distracting.

LAUREN: I think death is a lot more than a distraction. I think I am absolutely frozen with a kind of dread, a kind of anxiety to be surrounded by the idea of death like this, it's big, Kyle, and I don't want to die, I don't, I don't.

WALTER: That is heavy. Yeah.

JAMES: This play is about love, not death. This is a light-hearted comedy about love and we are going to look mighty silly against a backdrop of mortality, my friend.

KYLE: *(Fighting his own increasing anxiety.)* I know we can make this work. It's simply an obstacle, an emotional obstacle and I find that emotional obstacles create death. Depth. You see in love there is always an undercurrent of death there is a ghost of loves past and marriage my God marriage what is marriage about if not death, in a way, girding ourselves against dying alone, birth, marriage, birth, death the great cycle, ritual, you see it's connected in a big way so it's possible that in a fully realized production I would even choose, yes I might, I might even choose such a metaphoric backdrop, I might.

(Kyle is slightly freaked out.)

WALTER: Death is in the air.

JAMES: We can feel it.

WALTER: We can smell it.

LAUREN: It's true. I do. I smell death. Stay away from me, Death!

KYLE: This is not real death. This is fake death. Do you not have enough focus to ignore fake flimsy pseudo-death?

(Meanwhile, someone is in the coffin and gets out of it. This is the writer, unseen by the others. He watches them.)

LAUREN: Everything is real in theater because everything is fake so to us everything has to be real or, or what are the options, Kyle, what are the options you might as well say we are fake, is that what you're saying, Kyle?

JAMES: This is what we do, Kyle.

WALTER: This is who we are.

LAUREN: Are we fake?

JAMES: Living on the edge, an emotional edge, putting ourselves out there, and this is our reality, Kyle.

LAUREN: Am I? Fake?

JAMES: So don't tell me something isn't real because I have to feel that it is.

KYLE: Let's all do some deep breathing here.

(They do.)

WRITER: I wanted to write a love story, a sweet little thing, an ode to love and maybe, maybe I did. Kyle is in love with James, I think, and Lauren is in love with James, who is in love with James. Walter is probably in love with Lauren. No one is in love with me because I am the writer, a writer of a sweet little nothing about love that for reasons of economic reality must be set in a theater whose current production of *Funeral Parlor Blues* requires the fixed set of a funeral parlor onstage. I'm willing to go with that.

KYLE: All right everybody. Can we please die again?

(They look at him.)

KYLE: What? From the top, please.

LAUREN: I know. We can rewrite this, just a bit, in such a way that the death thing we are feeling will make sense.

WALTER: Death never makes sense.

JAMES: Maybe the writer could make the proposal happen in a funeral parlor after the death of my character's mother, from whom I was estranged. That's much more interesting. That's potent. I like that.

LAUREN: Get the writer, this is good, ask the writer to change the location and I think it's *my* character's mother, and I am despondent, and I want to break up with my boyfriend because now I see what's important and what isn't and he's been dicking me around, just dicking me around refusing to commit but then he comes in and proposes right here in the funeral parlor.

KYLE: The writer is unavailable to us.

JAMES: It's a small adjustment. We can add a few lines ourselves.

WALTER: Hold it. What happens to me? I'm the waiter. What will I be if it's no longer set in a café? You can't just treat me like some expendable . . . what . . . waiter? . . . after I've been a part of the process you may think I am expendable but no one is expendable no one is.

KYLE: Calm down, Walter, we're not changing anything.

WALTER: I have been around the block more than a few times and you kids I did Albee you know The Albee the original, and Shakespeare?

"The weariest and most loathed worldly life
That age, ache, penury, and imprisonment
Can lay on nature, is a paradise
To what we fear of death."

So when I say "a nice merlot for the lovely lady," there is a weight to that.

JAMES: As the funeral director, you'll have a lot more lines. Or the chaplain, you can be the chaplain and you can come out and marry us right before doing the funeral.

WALTER: Oh. Cool.

KYLE: We are not rewriting this play. Now please. The words, as they are written. From the top.

WRITER: Do they see me
Haunting them
Am I a ghost
Or not

LAUREN: People are getting shot every day innocent people are getting shot and I cannot do this scene with the image of weeping mothers in my head. This is what's in my head and we are doing this light-hearted little comedy and I am an actress, an actress with dreams and aspirations such as getting in *People* magazine, maybe in *Vogue.* I've always wanted to be in *Vogue* but I cannot be that actress person who's sitting next to a coffin, Kyle.

WALTER: Death is not an abstraction. Death is not a newspaper headline. Haven't any of you known death yet?

JAMES: I held her when she died, she tried to wag her tail one last time for me, to fill my need, and I cried, What is this about? Why does the world include, of all things, this thing, this taking away, this?

WRITER: Does it matter? Did it ever? Wanting words heard even then was I invisible even then? Did I hope to change that?

WALTER: My grandma was so wonderful I barely knew her does that sound like a contradiction? She was a wonderful lady and she died when I was six. Dear Gran, I miss your floppy hats and flowered dresses and the flap of skin under your arms that you let me play with.

WRITER: I'm invisible I tried to be here for a long time but now all that seems like a real waste of energy and time because all the while I was trying to be heard I was disappearing from life.

(Everyone gets a chill simultaneously as they stay to themselves.)

KYLE: The writer is dead. The writer is dead, you you you —

WRITER: — disappearing into the pages nobody wanted to read anyway —

KYLE: — people! And I promised the writer that I would that I would do this piece somehow.

JAMES: Dead?

WRITER: I left behind some pages and a few friends but really if not for those friends —

LAUREN: He's . . . he's dead?

WRITER: — none of the pages would be around anyway.

(They toss their scripts and back away, afraid.)

KYLE: Where is everyone going?

JAMES: We really can't deal with death right now.

KYLE: You, too, Walter?

WALTER: There is another play here, the ghost of another play or, like, whatever, but the thing is we feel like we are trampling on a ghost.

(The actors exit.)

KYLE: Okay. Fine. Brilliant. Re-cast. Obstacles are good. I love obstacles. I love an empty stage. Even with somebody else's set, it's got a certain need. To be filled. Always a good place to begin: Emptiness. Blankness. Shadows.

WRITER: A walking shadow. A poor player who struts and frets his hour . . .

(The Writer starts to leave the stage . . .)

KYLE: . . . and then is heard . . . no more.

(The Writer looks to Kyle. They seem to see each other for a moment. Blackout.)

END OF PLAY

THE OBIT

by Donna de Matteo

To Herbert Berghof, for the ongoing opportunity, inspiration, and magic

ORIGINAL PRODUCTION

The Obit was directed by Carol Rosenfeld with the following cast:

Nicole . . . . Amy Love
Nicky . . . . Adam Rose

PLAYWRIGHT'S BIOGRAPHY

Donna de Matteo teaches playwriting at the HB Studio and has taught Contemporary Theatre at The College of New Rochelle. Her numerous plays have been performed at The Roundabout Theatre, Theatre East, The Cape Playhouse, The WPA, The John Drew in East Hampton, The McCarter at Princeton, and the HB Playwrights Foundation. Some of the latter productions include *The Silver Fox,* directed by Herbert Berghof and starring Uta Hagen; *The Flip Side,* a finalist in the Susan Smith Blackburn Prize (1982); *Almost on a Runway,* starring Jerry Stiller; and *The Last American Convertible,* which was presented at The Carnegie Mellon New Play Festival (1996). Ms. de Matteo is featured in Contemporary Women Playwrights by Kathleen Betsko and Rachel Koenig. Her other achievements include her three children, Joe, Darren, and Drea, and her marriage to her husband, Al.

NOTE

The Obit is about the sudden death of a father and the subsequent birth of a new relationship between a brother and sister. The brother is illegitimate; the sister is not. The sentiment displayed in *The Obit* was taken from a full-length play-in-progress titled *The Heir Apparent,* which was to be directed by Herbert Berghof before his untimely death.

THE OBIT

The reception room in a Manhattan funeral parlor. The room is austere and does not promote comfort. Two velvet French chairs are lined up against one wall with a table lamp between them.

Nicole, a pretty girl of nineteen, is nervously pacing around the room. She is holding an ashtray while smoking a cigarette. Intermittently, she looks at her watch. She is wearing black slacks and a black silk man-tailored shirt.

As she hears footsteps approaching, she puts out the cigarette and tries to affect a cool air.

Nicky, a boy of thirteen, enters, totally out of breath. He is carrying a knapsack and is dressed in a navy blazer, gray slacks, a white rumpled shirt, loosened tie, and dirty sneakers.

NICKY: Man, I am so sorry I'm late, but when I got out of the train station, I couldn't find a cab, and then, when I finally found one, I asked the driver, this really cool Rasta guy, how much it would be to get crosstown, and when he told me at least ten bucks at this time of day, I decided to . . .

NICOLE: . . . Walk?

NICKY: . . . Run. I decided to run . . . I'm on the track team, you know?

NICOLE: No, I didn't know . . .

NICKY: *(Still out of breath.)* I'm an excellent runner . . .

NICOLE: You look like you're going to pass out.

NICKY: Shit! I still have to change my shoes!

NICOLE: Hey, just calm down! Chill out!

NICKY: *(Still trying to catch his breath.)* But my mother told me I had to be in and out of here in one hour.

NICOLE: And my mother won't be here till two. It's one-fifteen now, so you have forty-five minutes. How much time do you need to look at a dead body and say a prayer over it, so just sit down for five minutes so we can talk.

NICKY: Talk about what . . . ?

NICOLE: Sit.

NICKY: Okay. Okay.

(He plops himself down in a chair.)

NICOLE: Do you want some water?

NICKY: I have my own, thank you.

(He takes a bottle of water out of his jacket pocket and takes a slug.)

NICOLE: And by the way, I'm Nicole.

NICKY: . . . And I'm Nicholas, but everybody calls me Nicky.

NICOLE: *(Nervously.)* So, I guess we should shake hands or something?

(She extends her hand. He wipes his hand on his jacket and shakes her hand.)

NICKY: My hands are all sweaty.

NICOLE: Christ, how weird is this . . . to be meeting you under these circumstances?

NICKY: It's extremely weird.

NICOLE: Nicole and Nicholas. God bless your father. He was a world-class egotist and had absolutely no imagination when it came to naming children.

NICKY: He was your father, too . . .

NICOLE: Yeah, well . . . if you're referring to what it said in the Obit, my advice to you is, you shouldn't believe everything you read in the papers.

NICKY: *(He does not want to get into this.)* . . . What Obit?

NICOLE: The Obituary column?

NICKY: *(Denies that he knows anything about it.)* I don't know what you're talking about.

NICOLE: You don't.

NICKY: No.

(Nicole takes the newspaper out of her bag and opens it to the Obit page.)

NICOLE: I'm talking about this. Your father's obituary. *(Quotes the paper.)* "Nicholas Bari . . . Beloved husband of Rose, and loving father of Nicole . . ."

NICKY: *(Cuts her off.)* I didn't read it.

NICOLE: *(She knows he is lying.)* You didn't?

NICKY: No.

NICOLE: Then why were you so upset when your name wasn't mentioned in it? *(A pause.)*

NICKY: *(Defensive.)* Upset? Why the hell should I be upset 'cause my name isn't mentioned in some stupid newspaper with a bunch of dead people?

NICOLE: So, then, you did read it?

NICKY: Maybe I did. Maybe I didn't, and anyway, who gives a shit about it? I gotta change my shoes. *(He goes to his knapsack and takes out his loafers. Then, starts to take off his sneakers.)*

NICOLE: *(Looks at her watch.)* You know, under any other circumstances, I'd be asking you silly questions like . . . "What do you want to be when you grow up? Are you into girls, yet?"

NICKY: I go to an all boys school, but yeah, I am into girls, not that I ever get to see any, but . . .

NICOLE: But unfortunately, we don't have the time for the normal things kids talk about, so let's cut right to the chase, Nicky, and stop the bullshit . . . I know all about that little stunt you pulled at your school after you read or didn't read the Obit you claim you don't give a rat's ass about . . .

NICKY: I didn't say rat's ass . . .

NICOLE: And don't change the subject . . . Your mother, my father's what should I call her, Nicky . . . Mistress? Cumare? Girlfriend . . . of fifteen years, phoned my house yesterday, My house where My mother lives, to beg me to let you come here today, and Thank God she got me on the phone and not my mother, who was too spazzed out on Valium over the death of her beloved husband. AND . . . your mother proceeded to tell me . . .

NICKY: My mother is a liar and a bitch. That's probably why he never married her.

NICOLE: He didn't marry her because he was married to my mother, but that is not the issue . . . what you did at school is . . .

NICKY: So, how come he never got divorced . . . ?

NICOLE: *(Loses her patience.)* How the hell do I know why he never got divorced? What do you want me to tell you? He was a Catholic . . . he was Italian . . . he was in the Mafia . . . he didn't believe in divorce. Murder, adultery, drug dealing, yes! Divorce, God Forbid!

NICKY: My mother said he wouldn't get divorced because of you . . .

NICOLE: You know, that man must've taken a trip to the Planet of the Apes to find these two women because your mother sounds just as dumb as mine. All married men say that so they never have to get married again . . . BUT . . . that is not your problem . . . *(A pause.)* . . . Trying to OFF yourself is . . .

NICKY: I did not try to OFF myself.

NICOLE: That's not what I heard . . .

NICKY: . . . I just went a little ballistic when my mother came up to school to tell me he had a heart attack. At first, I didn't believe her, so to prove it to me, she showed me the Obit . . . and . . .

NICOLE: . . . And what?

NICKY: . . . And when my name wasn't in it, maybe I did get pissed off, 'cause all I could think of was always having to make up stories, like when he would say he was coming to a track meet and never show up, or around the holidays when he couldn't be home while all of my other friends' dads were. And then, I kept thinking that the headmaster of my school might read it. He's one of those people who reads the Obituary column every morning with his coffee. And I knew once he read it, he'd know I was this little bastard, and before long, all the other kids would know it, too. And you know how those schools are, guys never stop teasing you about shit, so . . .

NICOLE: So . . .

NICKY: . . . So, I was standing with my mother on the campus when this big gust of wind came along and just whipped that fucking newspaper right out of her hand, and into the air, for everybody to see, so I just ran after it . . .

NICOLE: . . . You ran into the lake with all of your clothes on, Nicky . . .

NICKY: . . . I just kept following the newspaper flying, hoping I could just take that goddamn paper and burn it, and before I knew it, I was just floating around in the water till they dragged me out . . .

NICOLE: . . . And all of this over your name not being in an Obit? Do you really think anybody in your school or otherwise really gives a damn . . .

NICKY: *(Almost starts to cry.)* Maybe they don't, but I do . . . And I know I shouldn't have been thinking of such a stupid thing after hearing my father just died . . . but I was . . . and I feel really bad about it. I mean, he was my dad . . .

NICOLE: . . . And do you think, even for one lousy minute, that he was thinking about you when he died?

NICKY: I don't know . . .

NICOLE: . . . Want to know what I was thinking when I heard the news, Nicky?

NICKY: It couldn't have been as bad as what I was thinking . . . What?

NICOLE: *(Lights a cigarette.)* I was thinking of the day my mother decided to tell me about the affair my father was having with your mother. Of course I had no idea what an affair meant because I was six years old at the time. Somewhere in my mother's warped mind she thought that I, a first grader, could convince him to leave your mother. So, when I told my father what she told me, he told me she was crazy . . . And when I told her what he said, she decided to prove to me that she was not . . . nuts, that is . . . And so, that afternoon, when she picked me up from school, she walked me over to your mother's apartment . . . 900 Park Avenue was her address at the time . . . And, when I saw my father enter the building, my mother kept saying, "See, I'm not crazy." And, I said, "He's just going into the building," and she said, "Wait." . . . And we did . . . for the next two hours. My mother was crying, mascara was running down her cheeks, and she kept wiping it causing it to smear all over her face, and I kept telling her to stop cause people were staring at her. AND . . . when my father came out of the building with his arm cozily wrapped around your mother, who was very pregnant with you at the time . . . my mother proceeded to throw up right in the street. And, on that day, when I saw my father exit that building, I began praying like a good Catholic girl that my father should drop dead right on the spot. . . . So, when his friend came over to break the terrible news that he keeled over a crap table in Atlantic City, all I could think of, Nicky, is . . . Yes, there is a God, and he has finally answered my prayers.

(Nicole is blowing smoke rings into the air as Nicky stares at her. A pause.)

NICKY: Wow . . . that is a lot worse than what I was thinking.

NICOLE: I only told you that story so you wouldn't feel guilty.

NICKY: I only spoke to him the day before he died. Told him I needed new shoes . . . He told me to always buy shoes with rubber soles on them so they last longer . . .

NICOLE: . . . While his last request to his friends was to be laid out in a custom-made pair of alligator-tasseled loafers. That's who your father was, all show, and no substance, a man who looks good at weddings and funerals, so I wouldn't worry about your name not being in the Obit. If I had my way, my name wouldn't be there either. *(She picks up the paper and burns it with the lit cigarette.)* There. *(She looks at her watch.)* Let's go and see our father.

(She straightens out his tie as he tucks his shirt into his pants.)

NICKY: . . . Do you think . . . maybe . . . you could come and watch me run sometime . . . the guys at my school, they'll be so impressed . . .

NICOLE: You have a half an hour before my mother gets here . . . About your school, if you promise to stay out of the lake, maybe . . .

(The lights fade to black as they join hands and open the folding doors to view the casket. Blackout.)

END OF PLAY

THE LESSONS OF MY FATHER

by Catherine Filloux

For Odette Filloux and John Daggett

Original Production

The Lessons of My Father was directed by Jean Randich with the following cast:

Maurice . . . . Marvin Einhorn
Odile . . . . Dale Soules
Horse . . . . Molly Carden

Playwright's Biography

Catherine Filloux's new plays, *Silence of God* and *Mary and Myra,* premiered at Contemporary American Theater Festival (CATF) in 2002 and 2000. *Mary and Myra* also appeared at Todd Mountain Theater Project in 2002. Ms. Filloux is the 2003 James Thurber Playwright-in-Residence. She has been commissioned for a new play by Theatreworks/USA. She wrote the libretto for the opera *The Floating Box,* which received its world première at the reopening of Asia Society in 2001 (composer Jason Kao Hwang). Her first play, *Cut To: The Deal,* was produced in Theater X's 2002 season. Ms. Filloux is the winner of the 1999 Roger L. Stevens award from The Kennedy Center Fund for New American Plays for her play *Eyes of the Heart* and is the winner of the O'Neill's 1996 Eric Kocher Playwrights Award. She developed *Eyes* for Lifetime TV. *Photographs from S-21*, from the "The Museum Plays," was a finalist for the 1999 Heideman Award at Actors Theatre of Louisville and is the winner of the 1999 Nausicaa Franco-American Play Contest; it has been produced in Paris, England, Phnom Penh, and around the United States. *Storks* was produced at HB Playwrights Foundation and in the Immigrants' Theater Project's "Women without Borders Festival" at the Lower East Side Tenement Museum Theater. *Lessons of My Father* was part of "The Funeral Plays," at HB Playwrights. *The Sun Always Rose* was in "New Georges: Watch This Space," at HERE. *The Price of Madness* was produced by Emerging Artists at INTAR on Theatre Row; *Three Continents* appeared at New Georges; and *The Russian Doll* at Lincoln Center Theater Directors Lab. *White Trash* (1997 Heideman finalist), *Accepting Applause,* and *Converting* were staged at the Women's Project. *All Dressed Up and Nowhere to Go* and *Venus in the Birdbath* were produced in Baltimore and Buffalo. Ms. Filloux has developed an oral history project, *A Circle of Grace,* with the Cambodian Women's Group at St. Rita's Refugee Center in Bronx, New York. She was awarded a 2001 Artist's Residency Grant from the Asian Cultural Council for playwriting in Phnom Penh, Cambodia. She received her French baccalaureate in Toulon, France, and her MFA from the Dramatic Writing Program at New York University. She is a member of New Dramatists.

CHARACTERS

ODILE, a *pied noir,* French-Algerian woman.

MAURICE, her father.

HORSE, Odile as a girl.

PLACE

France.

TIME

Present.

THE LESSONS OF MY FATHER

Maurice lies in hushed stillness in his coffin. Odile enters, uncomfortable in elegant clothing, taking a Clementine from her pocket. A clock, marking time, chimes.

ODILE: Papa . . . Papa . . . in ten minutes they will take you to the church . . . For your sake I'm trying not to look pious and hypocritical. *(Adjusting her expression.)* It's hard. *(Looking at the Clementine.)* For you, just like in Heaven.

(She waits, looking at him closely.)

ODILE: Your joke, your Tall Tale? . . . You invite everyone to the funeral and have the last laugh . . . Aren't you going to surprise me?

(She puts the Clementine in her pocket and starts to exit.)

ODILE: I knew I shouldn't have trusted you.

(Horse, Odile as a girl, runs past her, looking at creatures lying on the floor.)

HORSE: Papa, papa! Come here! What happened to the tadpoles? *(Picking up a creature.)* What is it . . . ?

ODILE: A frog.

HORSE: The tadpoles turned to frogs while we were sleeping . . . !

(Maurice bolts upright in his coffin, his younger self.)

MAURICE: And leaped out of their bowl. *(To Odile.)* As any normal frog would do.

(Horse gathers the creatures in her skirt.)

HORSE: But what's happened to them?

ODILE: They dried up.

HORSE: Outside of their water home. I'll put them in the ice chest, the cold will bring them back to life, I know it. They're so tiny . . .

MAURICE: My Horse . . .

HORSE: I must hurry.

MAURICE: I'm afraid the freezer will not resurrect them.

ODILE: They're dead.

HORSE: Dead, Papa?

MAURICE: Yes.

HORSE: Is it for good?

MAURICE: Yes, for good. Now, *you* are a brave person, my Horse. Death isn't necessarily so bad. Sometimes, you have to laugh in the face of it. *(He laughs with glee.)*

ODILE: Laugh?

MAURICE: They're all so pious at those funerals! And so hypocritical! You know what I'd love to do?

HORSE: No.

ODILE: Yes.

MAURICE: Run an announcement of my death in the Oran paper with the date and time of the wake at our house. All the people will arrive with their gloomy, lugubrious faces. *(Miming.)* Your mother will lead them solemnly into the living room and then when they're all here, I'll enter, straight and dignified, like this. They'll be left flabbergasted, and I'll have the laugh of my life! The last laugh. *(Laughing.)* Eh? What do you think? Not bad, huh? . . .

(Horse giggles.)

ODILE: It's not *real.*

HORSE: Maman would never agree to let you play the trick.

MAURICE: Here, in Algeria, the *story* is what is important, my Horse, not the reality. It's what we call a *galéjade.* A Tall Tale. You embellish it to fit the occasion. *(To Odile.)* A good laugh is always more important than anything else. Right?

ODILE: A good laugh, Papa? I'm nothing like you taught me to be.

(Maurice beckons to Horse, looking down into a hole as we hear turbulent sea rushing into the hole with a loud, sucking sound.)

MAURICE: Now, would you be afraid to go down there?

HORSE: Yes, very afraid, Papa.

MAURICE: Pofft, there's nothing to be afraid of. I'll take you down and then you can see for yourself.

ODILE: See what?

HORSE: What do you mean? How?

MAURICE: I'll hold you by your feet and lower you down, then you can have a real good look!

ODILE: At what?

MAURICE: You can do anything.

HORSE: I don't know.

MAURICE: I'll see to it you're not raised as a sissy, but the hard way, hardened to hardship. You must always trust me. I'm your father and I wouldn't wish anything dangerous for you . . . Don't you want to have a better look?

HORSE: Okay . . .

(He takes her by the feet and lowers her down into the hole.)

ODILE: Wait a minute.

MAURICE: Well, how is it down there? . . .

HORSE: I'll tell you in a second, I'm looking.

MAURICE: That's fine, just call when you're ready. *(To Odile.)* Take the time to have a real good look.

(After a moment.)

HORSE: Okay, pull me up.

(He pulls her out. She wipes spray from her face; Odile wipes tears.)

MAURICE: Didn't I tell you not to be afraid?

HORSE: Oh, Papa!

MAURICE: See? You can trust me.

ODILE: No.

MAURICE: Always remember, there is no difference between a boy and a girl and what they're capable of doing.

ODILE: No difference. How could you truly say that? What were you thinking?

(She adjusts her tight-fitting clothes. Horse picks up a schoolbag and starts to run away. Maurice delivers the scene to Odile.)

MAURICE: Where are you going, my Horse? Rushing in, out of breath. What happened?

HORSE: Nothing.

ODILE: I was at Lise's.

MAURICE: What were you doing?

HORSE: Homework.

ODILE: Lise had to leave.

MAURICE: Did something happen you're not telling me?

ODILE: Yes, Papa.

MAURICE: What?

HORSE: I don't want to talk about it right now.

MAURICE: Maybe you'll feel better if you say it. You know, you can trust me.

ODILE: I can't.

HORSE: I'm going to finish my homework . . .

MAURICE: Look what I brought home from the harbor? A whole big stalk of bananas. You can pretend you're in the jungle and each time you pass it grab a banana to eat. Have fun! They can only be good for you. I couldn't resist buying them just to see your reaction!

HORSE: Lise's father came into the room while I was studying . . .

MAURICE: Go on . . .

ODILE: Alone. He began to . . . I didn't know what to do. I was ashamed.

HORSE: He leaned over my chair where I was sitting and . . . He put his hand under and all over . . .

MAURICE: It's good you ran away. How did you do it?

HORSE: He moved, to the door . . .

ODILE: To lock it.

HORSE: I quickly got up from my chair. Ran from the house.

MAURICE: You're a brave and smart girl. I'm proud of you.

ODILE: Why?

MAURICE: Listen to me carefully, my Horse.

HORSE: Did I do wrong?

MAURICE: Most men are not like your friend's father. They're decent and would never do such a thing, but there are a few like him and because of them you need to be extra careful as a girl.

ODILE: I didn't know.

MAURICE: Of course not, Odile. It was very bad of him to do what he did. Parents' faults fall back on their own children. You can see why I'm going to ask you not to go to your friend's anymore.

HORSE: Yes . . .

MAURICE: Take a banana.

ODILE: I'm not hungry.

(Maurice, Odile, and Horse face the audience.)

MAURICE: I went to see that man! Slapped him hard across the face.

(Odile makes the motion of slapping.)

ODILE: Just keep quiet. You know why I'm doing this. Don't ever do such a thing again and if you speak against me for what I just did, I promise in tomorrow's paper your actions towards my daughter will be spelled out in detail.

HORSE: You called him a . . .

HORSE/ODILE/MAURICE: Bastard!

(Odile takes the Clementine from her pocket and gives it to Maurice.)

MAURICE: I always thought Heaven would be lined with Clementine trees and you could help yourself to as many as you wanted!

ODILE: Papa, we used to ride our bikes to the orchards. There was a priest, Father Clement, who invented the hybrid tangerine?

(The clock chimes the hour. He gives back the Clementine.)

ODILE: I must tell you good-bye now. I can't breathe.

(Bright sunlight as Horse shouts.)

HORSE: We're at the top of the mountain, Papa!

MAURICE: Look at the sea, my Horse! There is the harbor of Mers-El-Kébir and, see, in the distance, Ain-El-Turk where you go swimming? Now, I must teach you how to breathe.

(He swells his chest with obvious pleasure.)

MAURICE: You throw out your chest like this . . . fill your lungs and take a deep breath . . . Now exhale!

(He makes a powerful blowing sound as he exhales.)

MAURICE: In order to live well, Odile, all you have to do is learn to breathe. Not just with your body, but with your soul. Passionately. You never let things happen to you.

ODILE: *You* make them happen . . .

MAURICE: *You* make them happen. Throw out your chest . . .

(Maurice and Horse swell their chests.)

HORSE: . . . I am . . .

MAURICE: Fill your lungs . . .

HORSE: . . . I'm filling them . . .

MAURICE: Take a deep breath . . .

(They take deep breaths.)

MAURICE: Now exhale through your mouth!

(They exhale, making a powerful blowing sound.)

HORSE: It makes me dizzy, Papa!

MAURICE: With me here, you won't fall.

(The clock chimes again. Horse combs Maurice's hair with her fingers.)

ODILE: To start is, never to end . . . Along the roads of Oran are the telephone poles your own father installed. Who uses the phones now? Your mother a seamstress takes you a little boy to the factory, sets you on the table, the seamstresses play with you, teach you to love women. You bring me home tadpoles and a baby stork. At the harbor you look for what is cheap to make us laugh. Your brother flying across the Mediterranean, killed in a fog crash, plane goes down. From that day — the day you and I go to identify his body — you never shave your beard or moustache. Until today when they shave it for you because you are dead.

MAURICE: In order to live well, my Horse . . .

ODILE: Every piece of history dies, the smoke of the cigarillos you used to smoke, which made your moustache yellow, your laugh, the revolver you kept in your night table, your daughter, they will lower the lid of the coffin and I will never. Never see . . . See . . . Never see you . . .

MAURICE: All you have to do is . . .

ODILE: *(She sticks out her tongue.)* Ahhhggghhh. I'm sick. Langue. Long. French-English-French-English . . .

MAURICE: Learn to breathe . . .

ODILE: I'll go back to the country where I live. I'll speak English. My tongue can't wrap itself around the words so I'll stutter. Look inside, see my throat. I'm sick. The lessons of my father . . .

MAURICE: Not just with your body . . .

ODILE: I'm almost there, you're almost, they will lower . . .

MAURICE: But with your soul. Passionately. You never let things happen to you . . .

ODILE: Where you are going there are no phones . . .

MAURICE: *You* make them happen . . .

ODILE: Cannot reach you, cannot reach you . . .

MAURICE: Throw out your chest . . .

(Maurice swells his chest.)

ODILE: They will lower, they will lower, the phone lines installed by your own . . .

MAURICE: Fill your lungs. Take a deep breath . . .

(He takes a deep breath.)

MAURICE: Now exhale through your mouth!

(He exhales, making a powerful blowing sound. She doesn't exhale.)

ODILE: They will lower the lid.

MAURICE/HORSE: You won't fall.

(Maurice lies back down in his coffin. Odile tries to sing him a song, "Valentine," but says Clementine instead. She places the Clementine in the coffin. Horse swells her chest with obvious pleasure.)

HORSE: In order to live well, all you have to do is learn to breathe. Not just with your body, but with your soul. Passionately. You never let things happen to you. *You* make them happen. Throw out your chest.

(Odile unbuttons her suit jacket and throws out her chest.)

HORSE: Fill your lungs. Take a deep breath. Now exhale through your mouth! With me here, you won't fall.

(Horse takes Odile's hand. They breathe in together then exhale.)

END OF PLAY

RESCUE AT THE MOMENT OF DEATH

by Alexandra Gersten-Vassilaros

Original Production

Rescue at the Moment of Death was originally produced at the HB Playwrights Theatre in June 2000; directed by Caroline Kava with the following cast:

Jill . . . . Tami Dixon
Dennis . . . . Peter Jensen

RESCUE AT THE MOMENT OF DEATH

A funeral parlor in a New York suburb. Jill, a woman in her late twenties, kneels beside a coffin. A man in his early forties steps quietly into the room. She is startled.

DENNIS: It's all right. We don't have to acknowledge each other.

JILL: You just did.

DENNIS: I'm sorry.

JILL: Now what do we do? This is weird.

DENNIS: I felt I had to come. *(She approaches the coffin.)* I saw it all in the papers.

JILL: *(She nods, tearful.)* He was about to retire in two weeks. He wanted a new car. Just left the Ford dealership, a new blue Explorer, drove a coupla blocks, and there's a fire, smoke, screaming people hanging out windows. Coulda called his ladder company. No, he runs in, pulled out two tots, a mom. In his arms, you know. Could you have done that?

DENNIS: *(Carefully.)* Well, I'm not a fireman, am I?

JILL: So, he runs back in. Then the chimney collapsed, the roof. Toppling. Bricks and roof and smoke. Underneath, my dad.

DENNIS: I'm so sorry.

JILL: He wasn't around for me but BOY WAS HE AROUND FOR OTHERS! Saved lives! *Fuck you, Dad.*

DENNIS: It's all right to be angry.

JILL: I hate this! I'm mad at death. I'm sad and mad he saved lives besides mine! HE WOULDN'T EVEN LOAN ME MONEY FOR RENT.

DENNIS: I know.

JILL: I have to get it out, huh? Otherwise it makes you sick, doesn't it? You know how much I kept things in. How much I tried to handle everything, all the crazy balls in the air all the time the best I could. Now I feel like I'm exploding all over the place. I don't mean to talk to you this way. So blurting everything out like this.

DENNIS: Your anguish is to be expected.

JILL: Anguish, yeah, good point. Oh and I'm off my mood inhibitors. I just didn't see the good of being, uh, inhibited, especially at a time like this. That's okay. Don't you think?

DENNIS: You're learning to be comfortable with your own decisions.

JILL: *(She starts to cry.)* Am I? I hope so. The mayor's supposed to be coming tomorrow to lay the Wreath of a Hero at the gravesite. There's gonna be photographers snapping up pictures. Do I smile? *(She smiles.)* Do I frown? *(She frowns.)* Just blank? *(She looks ahead blankly.)* I don't know, I need advice about a lot of things, I guess, and seeing you I can't help but think maybe we should pick up where we left off. *(He doesn't seem happy about that idea.)* Nah, right? The way we ended was weird. You were thinking about the way we ended, right?

DENNIS: Well, it was surprising.

JILL: Yeah.

DENNIS: It was abrupt.

JILL: The way I just walked out.

DENNIS: It hadn't ever happened to me just that way before. And then never hearing from you —

JILL: Can I be totally honest —

DENNIS: Can you? Of course.

JILL: I'd actually been feeling that for months we were going over and over the same territory again and again and again.

DENNIS: Why didn't you feel that you could say something?

JILL: I figured that's probably what therapy is, right?

DENNIS: Well, yes but —

JILL: Plus I think I craved your, your . . . what?

DENNIS: My *what?*

JILL: The way you looked at me inside. It made me feel held together, organized. Not so splattered all the time, like now? *(She panics a little.)* I just feel so, shaky and tiny —

DENNIS: Jill.

JILL: Teeny in the face of all that's happened —

DENNIS: Jill.

JILL: — wandering in the dark. The total dark.

DENNIS: I have to stop you.

JILL: Stop me?

DENNIS: *(Abruptly.) I'm sorry,* this just isn't appropriate.

JILL: It's not? What's not?

DENNIS: I can't consult with you —

JILL: Oh. I thought you were just listening.

DENNIS: I realize that you are falling apart, Jill.

JILL: I am?

DENNIS: And that's to be expected —

JILL: Falling apart?

DENNIS: Yes, but the *issue* is, which you've needed to ignore, I don't know why really, but but the *issue* is that I am usually uh, *paid, paid* for my expertise. I'm a *P-H-D.* I'm a *graduate* of Columbia, *cum* laude, a member of the board, the Board of Psychiatric Medicine —

(Note: Overlap next two speeches of Dennis and Jill.)

JILL: *(Disbelieving his nerve.)* My dad burned to a — I don't — I don't — My dad's in there! He's dead. Okay? Dead!!

DENNIS: I have credentials up and down my wall. My training and achievements, my *dedication* moreover entitles me to ask to, to *demand* really — *(Overlap ends on:)* I'm not comfortable — I'm sorry.

(He hands her a white envelope.)

JILL: What's that?

DENNIS: It's for you.

JILL: You didn't have to write a — *(Opening it, she's shocked.)*

DENNIS: You can't go through life leaving trails of —

JILL: It's a bill. Dennis, it's a fucking bill!

DENNIS: I should *never* have allowed you to call me by my first name.

JILL: You bring a bill to a wake???

DENNIS: You never left a forwarding address! How was I supposed to find you?

JILL: Whaddya check the obits for patients who owe you money?

DENNIS: You're five years past due!

JILL: I don't believe you!

DENNIS: Look, I'm sorry, but *I deserve to be paid, don't I?* I wasn't helping you for *free!*

JILL: You want me to what, like race to the bank machine with a wad of cried-out tissue in my hand and withdraw ten thousand dollars??? Are you nuts?!

DENNIS: A check. Can't you just write a check??

JILL: When did I ever have that kind of money?

DENNIS: Isn't there insurance? A city pension?

JILL: Not yet! Fucking Christ. I mean, you come to a funeral parlor and and and, try to mug me for a bill from years and years ago.

DENNIS: Mug you? Bills don't just go away. They don't disintegrate with time.

JILL: Talk about inappropriate!

DENNIS: Self-command is an elegance I strive for so from this point on I'm going to restrain myself . . . but but, look, *bottom line,* bottom line, *the bottom fucking line* is that you owe me a lot of fucking money.

JILL: Wait a second!

DENNIS: You were with me for six years, Jill!

JILL: I paid the first two. I paid!

DENNIS: The first two you paid in full.

JILL: And then we, c'mon, agreed —

DENNIS: Partial payment for the next two and —

JILL: But, wait a second —

DENNIS: Let me finish! The last *two years* you paid me nothing. *Nothing.*

JILL: I had no *job!* I was fired from Barney's for stealing men's cologne for Father's Day.

DENNIS: I remember all that, so I generously —

JILL: Took advantage —

DENNIS: Wait, what? I took what? What?

JILL: Advantage.

DENNIS: How did I do that?

JILL: You let me *talk.*

DENNIS: I let you what?

JILL: Talk and talk and talk my head off! I mean, what was my *big* issue?

DENNIS: I remember many issues, Jill.

JILL: The *big* one. The big one! Debt. *Debt.*

DENNIS: You don't start out in therapy talking about *debt* — you start with direct causal relationships.

JILL: But *six years* on my mother and father!? I had *rent* to pay. I had credit card debt. Laundry debt. Meantime ching ching ching my therapy bill is becoming a goddamn monkey on my back —

DENNIS: Wait a second!

JILL: — and the monkey was saying "GET OFF THE COUCH, YOUR THERAPIST IS A THIEF!"

DENNIS: *You owe me ten thousand dollars. I need it to live!!!*

JILL: Whaddya need a brilliant mind to figure out that a debtor shouldn't run a fucking endless tab?

DENNIS: I did it for you. I did it for *you!!*

JILL: You enabled me, Dennis. You enabled me!

DENNIS: *(Anguished.)* I was helping you, you twit! You graceless narcissist. You hapless user, God! You don't know it, do you, but you've learned to manipulate to get attention. Don't you see? The debt your father and mother owe to you is the debt you owe to me — don't you see the cycle repeating itself????

JILL: How do my father and mother figure into this?

DENNIS: Your your mother's a nut! You you were an unwanted child. When she found out she was pregnant with you she tried to kill your *brother,* who became an obsessive compulsive *tongue chewer.* He locked you in the boiler room when you were ten and nobody knew you were gone for *weeks!* Your *father* was an absent workaholic with a crazy temper at home but but now he's going to be remembered as a hero firefighter. That that makes you a victim, Jill.

JILL: Wow. You remembered everything.

DENNIS: I'm a sap is what I am. *(Anguished.)* Goddamnit. I, I see a woman like you and in spite of hearing alarms, sirens screaming, first-alert warning systems roaring, blaring in my ears, instead of running away from people like you, far far away, I *marry* you. I take you on as clients. I walk your dog. I lick your shoes. I throw myself down like a twenty-four hour moving sidewalk to any any any fucked-up victim I see, why? Because, I want to help you. I want to help all of you!

JILL: Oh my God. Dennis. Oh my God. You were trying to rescue me, weren't you?

DENNIS: Look, my wife's in love with someone else. She wants a divorce. I need to find a place to live. I'm sleeping in my office. I have ten clients like you I let slack on payments. I can't sleep. I can't eat. I can't think — I don't know anything anymore except except I'm a sap-chump. So do me a favor, I don't want money, you have no fucking money anyway, I just need to rest. I'm so tired. I could get in the coffin, okay? Two for one, no one will know, I'm dead already. I'll clear all your debt if you'll just just —

JILL: Shhhhh. *(She hugs him, concerned.)*

DENNIS: I'm very upset. *(Near tears.)*

JILL: You need to rest.

DENNIS: *(The injustice of life pummels him.)* The guy's a friend of mine!

JILL: Shhhhh.

DENNIS: He's living at my place. He's there now. Can you believe that?

JILL: It's all going to be okay.

DENNIS: My mother used to say that.

JILL: And didn't she make it better?

DENNIS: No. Never. Not once. Ever.

JILL: It's okay. You'll see. I want to help you. Let me help you. *(She leads him to a row of chairs, she sits one row behind him.)*

DENNIS: Are you, are you going to *pay* me?

JILL: *(Sincerely.)* No. You'll talk. I'll listen.

(As Dennis lies across a row of mourner's chairs. Lights fade.)

END OF PLAY

TIGHTWAD
An Operetta

story and lyrics by Dmitry Lipkin
music by Tony Angeles

To Colette, God I love that girl

ORIGINAL PRODUCTION

The Tightwad was directed by Oleg Kheyfets with the following cast:

Fenimore	Jim Cyrus
Abigail	Gin Hammond
Ismene	Betsy Worth McKibbon
Lucian	Pedro Porro
Sven	Drew Battles
Little Leah	Stephanie Ansin
The Gypsy	Valerie Stanford

PLAYWRIGHT'S BIOGRAPHY

Dmitry Lipkin was born in Moscow and emigrated to Louisiana at age eleven. His plays include *Cranes* (produced by The New Group, 1999), *Skitaletz, "The Wanderer"* (O'Neill National Playwrights Conference, 2000), *Moscow Nights* (A Contemporary Theatre, Seattle, 2000), *Baton Rouge* (EST), *The Elephant Play* (Playwrights' Collective, Printer's Devil Theatre), *Pithecus, I Am Laika,* and *The Tightwad,* (HB Playwrights), *A Forest of Stone, My Job is My Life* ("Chekhov Now" Festival, NYC 2000), and *Incident at Dental Clinic #44* (a screenplay for Fox/Searchlight). Mr. Lipkin is a recent alumnus of New Dramatists, an MFA graduate from NYU, a past Van Lier Fellow at Manhattan Theatre Club, and the 2000 Bug 'n Bub award-winner from Primary Stages. He has taught playwriting at NYU and is a co-founder of The Playwrights' Collective (1990–1998), with whom he produced a ton of new work off-off-Broadway in a very small room. After finishing his play *The Poet's Hour,* Mr. Lipkin spent most of 2002 in southern Mexico where he studied Spanish, wrote his new play *Total America,* and ate a whole lot of avocados.

CHARACTERS

FENIMORE, the deceased.
ABIGAIL, his older daughter.
ISMENE, his younger daughter.
LUCIAN, his son.
SVEN, Abigail's husband.
LITTLE LEAH, Abigail's and Sven's daughter.
THE GYPSY

NOTE

The Tightwad is best played "fast and dry." It's funny. It's a musical about reviving a dead guy for money.

THE TIGHTWAD

Fenimore's house, before the wake. Fenimore, the deceased, lies in an open coffin, peaceful. His progeny rummages through the house, searching for something with silent desperation. Little Leah sits off to the side. They sing, a cappella, turning away from the casket.

ABIGAIL: *Father was a rich man.*
LUCIAN: *But he was a cheapskate.*
ISMENE: *Wouldn't give an inch, man.*
SVEN: *Ditched us like an ingrate.*

(Lights shift revealing a piano behind the scrim. Music begins as they search the boxes, memories of life with Dad fully flooding back and overtaking them . . .)

ALL FOUR: *Father was a rich man*
But he was a cheapskate
Wouldn't give an inch, man
Ditched us like an ingrate

(The casket shakes. Only Little Leah sees it.)

LITTLE LEAH: Mommy!
ABIGAIL: — Sh — sh.

(The shaking stops. The other three hum as Lucian sings.)

LUCIAN: *When I was a little boy*
Mother bought a brand new toy
"Come now Lucian, play my pet
With the new erector set"
When I was asleep that prick
Stole my pieces brick by brick
Sold my Legos at the store
For a pack of Menthol Mores

ALL FOUR: *Father was a rich man*
But he was a cheapskate
Wouldn't give an inch, man
Ditched us like an ingrate

(The casket shakes with more vigor.)

LITTLE LEAH: Daddy!
SVEN: — Sh — sh

(The shaking stops. The three hum as Ismene sings.)

ISMENE: *When I was but seventeen*
Prep school voted me a queen
And to make the local press
All I needed was a dress
Daddy took the dough I saved
Spent it on some stock he craved
I came naked to the prom
Every boy was Peeping Tom . . . !

ALL FOUR: *Father was a rich man*
But he was a cheapskate
Wouldn't give an inch, man
Ditched us like an ingrate
(Fenimore's foot goes up involuntarily.)

LITTLE LEAH: Mommy! Daddy!

ABIGAIL AND SVEN: — Sh — sh — sh!

(The foot falls back down. The three hum as Sven sings, stiff and hesitant.)

SVEN: *I don't have that . . . much to say*
Kept my in-laws . . . far at bay
Still I shudder . . . when I hear
What he did for . . . his career
How he stole and . . . cheated blind
Every man and . . . womankind
Hope the bastard . . . rots in hell
Tortured in his . . . private cell

(Sven walks away, worked up. At this point, as if in response to Sven, Fenimore's hand jerks out of the casket, stiffly grasping. Little Leah sees him, aghast.)

ALL FOUR: *Father was a rich man*
But he was a cheapskate
Wouldn't give an inch, man
Ditched us like an ingrate

LITTLE LEAH: Papa, mama — look!

ALL FOUR: Sh — sh — sh — sh!

LUCIAN: Shut up, little girl.

(The hand falls back. Abigail sings, gentle and just.)

ABIGAIL: *What the others said was right*
Father's wad was very tight
Still I think maybe I might
Gently speak of him tonight
Maybe he'd have seen the light

Climbed up to a moral height
Known the wrong deeds from the right
If he only had some . . . sight . . .
(Speaks.) Foresight insight — any sight . . . !

THE OTHER THREE: *But he didn't have the sight . . .*
No, he never saw the light

ALL FOUR: *(Finding the old rhythm.) Father was a rich man*
But he was a cheapskate
Wouldn't give an inch, man
Ditched us like an ingrate
(Faster.)
Cheated at Monopoly
Cheated at Parcheesi
Tried to cheat the lottery
But it wasn't easy
(As the pace gets faster and faster, Fenimore's hand comes out of the casket, grasping at the wood.)

ISMENE: *Cheated us at pitch and toss*

LUCIAN: *Bingo and casino*

ABIGAIL: *Pinball poker chess lacrosse*

SVEN: *And the game of keno*

WOMEN: *Cheated us at duck duck goose*

MEN: *Scrabble, Shoots and Ladders*

WOMEN: *Played the board games fast and loose*

MEN: *Not that it all matters*

ALL FOUR: *Cheated like a cheater does*
Cheated like a chicken
Told the children Santa Claus

ISMENE: *With a stroke was stricken*

ALL FOUR: *But the most important cheat*

ABIGAIL: *(Shows a picture of her sainted mother.) Cheated that man on his wife*

ALL FOUR: *With his plastic car complete*

ABIGAIL: *He cheated at the Game of Life*

ALL FOUR: *Yes he . . . cheated at the Game . . . of Life . . .!*
(At the climactic finish, Little Leah, who has been tugging at her parents and relatives, points screaming —)

LITTLE LEAH: MOMMY DADDY LOOK!!
(They turn around, gasping. Fenimore's hands stiffen . . .)

ABIGAIL: My God.

(Silence. The Gypsy appears, holding two vials with red and green liquid. She approaches the casket, bending Fenimore's limbs, checking his eyes, tongue, etc. The others watch, confused and scared.)

THE GYPSY: The tongue too stiff. The limb too hard.

ABIGAIL: *(Stepping out, shy.)* I'm sorry . . . But the wake is not till eight.

THE GYPSY: The tongue too stiff! — The limb too hard!

(Abigail backs away. The Gypsy looks at her vials.)

ABIGAIL: Are you . . . on the guest list?

LUCIAN: *(Through his teeth.)* I don't think she's on the guest list.

THE GYPSY: My potion wrong. Need chro-mium . . . ura-nium . . . I will combine!

(She mixes something behind her back. Sven steps out.)

SVEN: Dear madam, pardon for the question but . . .

ISMENE: Who are you?

ABIGAIL: . . . To our dearly dead, that is?

(Pause. Something smokes behind the Gypsy's back.)

THE GYPSY: . . . Nobody said?

SVEN: . . . No.

THE GYPSY: Playboy never said . . . he hired me?!

ABIGAIL: "Hired"? . . . For what?

THE GYPSY: To find the money.

(They look at Lucian, standing to the side, embarrassed.)

ISMENE: Lucian? You're friends with this itinerant?

LUCIAN: *(Through his teeth.)* . . . I thought we had agreed to do it afterwards.

THE GYPSY: After too late! . .. The tongue too big! . . . The brain — too soft. He drink it now he will tell you everything.

ABIGAIL: You mean . . . our father will come back to life . . . ?

THE GYPSY: No! Not to life! We make him zombie for a little bit!

ABIGAIL: A zombie. God.

THE GYPSY: You want the money, no?!

SVEN: We do.

THE GYPSY: And dead man left you nothing!

ISMENE: Like an ingrate. Yes.

THE GYPSY: So I give dead man little pep — he tell you where the money's hid! . . . I take a little off the top and everybody happy, no?

SVEN: Yes. Everybody happy. Yes.

ISMENE: I don't believe this scam.

THE GYPSY: A scam! . . . You! You call me a scam?!

(Approaches Ismene, pissed off, as music begins.)

ABIGAIL: Forgive us for our sister, please. She . . . has an irrational fear of itinerant gypsies. It's a real phobia . . . ! It's truly been diagnosed . . . !

(The Gypsy sings, at first to Ismene, who tries to turn away from her, irrationally fearful.)

THE GYPSY: *When I cured the Queen of Sheba*
Back in old Addis Abeba
Never once did she say that I was a scam

Or would ever poor old Sarah
Give birth to the Jewish era
If I didn't help her out with Abraham

Or the time the great Mohammed
Rode his ass and I got on it
And we took off to Medina on the lam

And I was a bit distracted
But I swear he really acted
Like I got him outta spiritual jam

So if you got any issue
Take a pill and take a tissue
And remember just exactly who I am

I'm the one who tutored Nietzsche
Told Medici he was peachy
And sold story rights to old . . . Omar Khayyám

ISMENE: *(Surly.)* Okay . . . Fine.

LUCIAN: So we'll do it then?

SVEN: Yes. Let's just get it over with.

(The Gypsy pinches Fenimore's cheeks, studying his face.)

ABIGAIL: This won't hurt our father, will it?

THE GYPSY: Nothing hurt the father! Father dead!

(She puts a finger in the greenish smoky liquid, tastes it cringing, then opens Fenimore's mouth.)

THE GYPSY: Drink Fenimore. Drink — this time potion good.

(She sings under her breath, pouring the potion into Fenimore's mouth as it dribbles down his chin.)

THE GYPSY: *I mix the right amount of geranium*

Uranium, mediterranium

(She pours the rest of potion into Fenimore, then shows the labels to different members of the family —)

THE GYPSY: *I put the right proportion of the —*

SVEN: *(Reads.)* Ginger root.

ABIGAIL: A pigeon foot.

LITTLE LEAH: . . . And tutti fruit?

(Fenimore belches in response.)

THE GYPSY: That's right.

And when I finish I puree it all (and then)
Sauté it all

ISMENE: . . . *In alcohol.*

THE GYPSY: *'Cause for a dead man it's a surest way*

LUCIAN: *To seize the day*

THE GYPSY AND LUCIAN: *And death delay.*

(Still prostate, Fenimore begins to shake and writhe.)

THE GYPSY: *And for a dead man it's the finest drug*

THE GYPSY, SVEN, AND LUCIAN: *To take a jug*

THE GYPSY, SVEN, AND ABIGAIL: *And chug-a-lug . . .*

ISMENE: . . . *And tell the living where he hid the money.*

(The music continues as Fenimore suddenly sits up in the casket. They gasp, slowly converging as he begins to babble to the music, his tongue stiff.)

FENIMORE: *Ba . . . ba . . . ba-ba . . . ba-ba-ba-ba . . . ba . . . ba . . . ba . . .*

(Then try to guess what he's referring to — "Bathroom? Basement? Box? Baden Baden?" — then, getting frustrated —)

ALL FOUR AND GYPSY: *And for the dead man it's the best of ends*
To make amends
In dividends
(Louder.)
Before the angel of our Lord descends
What did you do with all the money?
(Louder.)
What did you do with all the money?
(Louder, frustrated.)
Before the angel of our Lord descends
Tell us what you did with the money!!

(Fenimore looks around, confused, then, to no one in particular —)

FENIMORE: *Bicycle spoke*
When I awoke

A rain drop fell
Into a well

My mother said
To stay in bed
Two two is four
Or maybe more

ABIGAIL: *(Quiet.)* What is he doing?

THE GYPSY: He's remembering his childhood.

FENIMORE: *I am alone*
The bully's back
He holds a stone
He will attack

It is too late
I should have known
I am afraid
The stone is thrown
(Repeats the last line like an automaton.)
The stone is thrown, the stone is thrown, the stone is thrown . . .
(He continues, as the Gypsy slaps him around. The others sigh in frustration; then, under their breath —)

THE FOUR: *But for the dead man this is in the past*
His bed is made
His lot is cast
Before you're in the earth come tell us fast
What did you do with all the money?
(Fenimore gets out of the casket, approaches them, grasping at bits and pieces of his life. He sings, now more emotional, making his most meaningful contact with Little Leah —)

FENIMORE: *And I remember when the slant of light*
Came through my window in the night
And mother said I gave an awful fright
Afraid the ghost was there to take me

And all my evenings and my afternoons
I spend alone upon my island dunes
And cried and listened to my oldie tunes
Hoping the ghost won't come to take me

Now rigor mortis slowly setting in
I know it's time forever to begin
I loved my life but I know it's a sin
To spend it in the way I spent it

And when you tell me that I cheated blind
The Game of Life that treated me so kind
To you I say I hope you never find . . . !
(Slowly, growing stiff, he goes back into casket and lies down.)
The stony ghost . . . about to take me.
(He freezes stiff. They look at him in silence.)

ISMENE: But where's the money, Daddy.

LUCIAN: Ditched us once again.

ABIGAIL: Can you revive him still . . . ?

THE GYPSY: Too late. The brain too soft. No potion in the world will make him zombie anymore.

(They look at one another, sit down, deep in thought. A sober silence.)

SVEN: Now we will never know.

LUCIAN: Maybe he gave it all to charity.

(They share a laugh, then sing, softly, a cappella.)

ABIGAIL: *And for the living it's the worst of ends.*

ALL FOUR: *The future rends.*

SVEN: *No dividends.*

ABIGAIL: *As slowly angel of our Lord descends.*

ALL FOUR: *Upon the earth and all its creatures.*

(Pause. The Gypsy takes off her wig, looks at Little Leah, sad, like a funny game has just come to an end. They get up leaving.)

ABIGAIL: C'mon. Let's go get ready for the wake.

LITTLE LEAH: . . . I'll be right there, Mom.

ABIGAIL: Okay. Not too long though.

LITTLE LEAH: Not too long.

(The others leave. She approaches Fenimore, tries to revive him like the Gypsy. He doesn't stir. She gives him her toy monkey, then sits with her back to him and begins to sing . . .)

LITTLE LEAH: *You know I still love you, Grandpa*
Even though you're pretty scary
I don't care that you're a tightwad
Your love in my heart I'll carry
And when you wake up from slumber

Maybe this day . . . maybe later
We'll go in the park on Sunday
Singing funny songs together.
(Fenimore, rather suave and debonair now, sits up in the casket behind her. She doesn't see him.)

FENIMORE: *And when I wake up from slumber*
Maybe this day . . . maybe later

FENIMORE AND LITTLE LEAH: *We'll go in the park on Sunday.*
Singing funny songs . . . together . . . !

END OF PLAY

FUNERAL HOME

by Quincy Long

Original Production

Funeral Home was directed by Kathleen Dimmick at the HB Short Play Festival 2000 with the following cast:

Bernard . . . . Richmond Hoxie
Toby . . . . Larry Block
Barbara . . . . .Annette Hunt
McHenry . . . . Trevor A. Williams
Singers . . . . .Tilden Marbit and Alexander Mowbray Balme

Playwright's Biography

Quincy Long's most recent productions include *The Lively Lad,* presented by New York Stage and Film at the Powerhouse Theatre at Vassar, and Soho Rep's production of *The Year of the Baby. The Joy of Going Somewhere Definite,* commissioned by the Mark Taper Forum, won a 1996 Fund for New American Plays Award and has been produced by the Atlantic Theater Company, the Mark Taper Forum, the Magic Theatre, and others. Mr. Long has recently adapted the play for Icon Productions in Los Angeles and has also adapted another play, *Shaker Heights,* which was nominated for an Outer Circle Critic's Award, for Atlantic Films in New York City. Mr Long, who is from Warren, Ohio, and lives in New York City, was recently commissioned to write a play for Playwrights Horizons and for the Ensemble Studio Theatre/Sloan Foundation Science and Technology Project. He's a graduate of the Yale School of Drama and a member of the New Dramatists and the Ensemble Studio Theatre as well as the HB Playwrights Unit.

Characters

BERNARD
TOBY
BARBARA
MCHENRY
SINGER

Place

Bernard's parlor.

FUNERAL HOME

Bernard's parlor. Bedroom off right. Kitchen off left. Front door down right. The sound of hammering in bedroom. A knock at the door. Bernard enters from bedroom, carrying a hammer. He wears a shirt, tie, and work apron. Bernard opens front door. Toby enters, carrying a suit and shopping bag.

TOBY: *(Holding up suit.)* One suit.

BERNARD: Good man, Toby.

TOBY: Sized thirty-eight exactly.

BERNARD: Well done, sir.

TOBY: *(Holding up shopping bag.)* Shirt, necktie, underwear, hose and shoes.

BERNARD: Perfect. I would be obliged if you would take everything into the kitchen, please.

TOBY: Done, sir.

(A knock at the door.)

BERNARD: Oh, and answer the door, if you don't mind.

(Bernard exits into bedroom. Toby opens front door. Barbara enters.)

BARBARA: Forgive me, I'm early.

TOBY: And I'm Toby.

BARBARA: Hello, Toby.

TOBY: You are a friend of Bernard's, then?

BARBARA: Not at all. I am Barbara, a friend of Mr. Sullivan's.

TOBY: Who?

BARBARA: The deceased.

TOBY: Somebody has died?

BARBARA: Mr. Sullivan, yes.

TOBY: Don't believe I know the fellow — knew the fellow, no.

BARBARA: Oh, Mr. Sullivan was very much a gentleman. It could be said, in fact, that Mr. Sullivan died of gentlemanliness. "Let me," he would always say. "Allow me."

TOBY: *(Beat.)* Would you excuse me just a moment?

BARBARA: Certainly.

(Toby exits to kitchen. Bernard enters from bedroom in a jacket and tie.)

BERNARD: Hello, I'm Bernard.

BARBARA: Hello, Bernard. My name is Barbara. *(Beat.)* And I'd like to use the facilities if I might.

BERNARD: Of course.

BARBARA: I seem to have soiled myself.

BERNARD: Just through the bedroom and to the left, Barbara.

(Barbara exits into bedroom. Toby re-enters from kitchen.)

TOBY: Hello, Bernard?

BERNARD: Yes?

TOBY: There is a corpse in your kitchen.

BERNARD: That is Mr. Sullivan, yes.

TOBY: But I have recently been informed that Mr. Sullivan was a gentleman.

BERNARD: What are you suggesting, Toby?

TOBY: Why, this fellow is completely naked.

BERNARD: Well, I've been preparing him for his funeral celebration.

TOBY: Oh, he was a special friend?

BERNARD: No, I didn't know him at all, Toby.

TOBY: I see. *(Lowering voice.)* He is a suicide then?

(A knock at the door.)

BERNARD: Ah, the singer. If you would get Mr. Sullivan dressed, Toby.

TOBY: Very well.

(Toby exits to kitchen. Bernard opens door. McHenry enters.)

BERNARD: You are late.

MCHENRY: I beg your pardon.

BERNARD: You are my singer, are you not?

MCHENRY: I am McHenry, sir.

BERNARD: Oh. Oh my goodness.

MCHENRY: The building superintendent.

BERNARD: Of course you are.

MCHENRY: Don't often see me in a necktie, do you?

BERNARD: You must forgive me, McHenry. Wanting a singer, I saw a singer.

MCHENRY: Well, that's only natural, sir, but I don't sing. No, I come about the item in the stairwell.

BERNARD: Can't it remain there for the time being, McHenry?

MCHENRY: No, sir. Sorry, sir. Got to maintain proper egress.

BERNARD: Very well, then. Bring it in. Bring it in.

(McHenry exits parlor. Barbara re-enters from bedroom.)

BARBARA: There is an informal quality to your preparations, I see.

BERNARD: I am for simplicity in all things, yes.

BARBARA: The coffin in your bedroom is simplicity itself; but there will be a singer, I trust?

BERNARD: Indeed there will. A tyro, I am told.

BARBARA: Mr. Sullivan was a baritone. It came from down here in him. Down in his midsection. For a small man, he made an enormous sound.

BERNARD: I'm sure he did, yes.

BARBARA: *(Beat.)* And I seem to have soiled myself again.

(Barbara exits to bedroom. McHenry re-enters parlor with sheet-covered corpse on gurney.)

BERNARD: Into the kitchen, please.

MCHENRY: The kitchen, sir?

BERNARD: Yes, and given that you're dressed for the occasion, perhaps you might want to participate.

MCHENRY: Me, sir? In what?

BERNARD: Why, in a funeral service.

MCHENRY: *(Pointing to corpse.)* For this one?

BERNARD: *(Pointing to kitchen.)* For that one.

MCHENRY: There's another one?

BERNARD: And we could use another mourner to fill out the form.

MCHENRY: I don't know, sir. Wouldn't be nothing to offend a Christian man, would there?

BERNARD: Not at all.

MCHENRY: I'm off to my mother's, you know.

BERNARD: The proceedings will be as wholesome as they are brisk, I can assure you.

MCHENRY: Well, why not?

BERNARD: Excellent.

(Barbara re-enters from bedroom.)

BERNARD: Into the kitchen then, McHenry.

(McHenry exits into kitchen with gurney.)

BARBARA: I must say, you have about you an abiding air of mastery, Bernard.

BERNARD: I believe in being of use, Barbara, and within that mandate I enjoy a certain authority.

BARBARA: Mr. Sullivan would approve. A solemnly joyful little man, he was, with the most exquisite taste and habits. Do you know that he would never eat his popcorn before the feature began?

BERNARD: Really?

BARBARA: No, he would wait until the previews were over, even until the credits had run their course, before he would touch his popcorn. I asked him about this once, and he said to me, "Barbara, my dear, you are very, very observant." This thrilled me, of course. Later I came to understand Mr. Sullivan's popcorn habits as the basis of a complex spiritual discipline.

BERNARD: Indeed.

BARBARA: Which I have since adopted as my own. And I have found improvements in my life, Bernard. A sudden increase in my levels of tolerance and civility, for example.

(McHenry re-enters from kitchen.)

MCHENRY: All done, sir.

BERNARD: Thank you, McHenry.

MCHENRY: It's a cheerful atmosphere in there, I must say.

BERNARD: Would you give me a hand in the bedroom, please?

MCHENRY: Which one?

BERNARD: Which . . . ?

MCHENRY: Hand! Hah! *(Beat.)* Sorry. Sorry ma'am.

(Bernard and McHenry exit into bedroom. Toby enters from the kitchen.)

TOBY: Hello, Bernard?

BARBARA: Bernard is in the bedroom with someone, I believe.

TOBY: Really?

BARBARA: I'm most interested in your friend, Toby.

TOBY: Which friend is that?

BARBARA: Why, Bernard.

TOBY: Oh, but we are not friends, Barbara.

BARBARA: No?

TOBY: We merely went to school together.

BARBARA: Many friendships are formed at school, Toby. In fact, most friendships are so founded in my experience.

TOBY: Oh, do not think for a moment that I enjoy such a friendship with Bernard. No, Bernard is — I believe Bernard to be one of the foremost business intelligences of his generation. That is why I take on any chore he assigns me immediately and without question.

BARBARA: Yes, not since Mr. Sullivan have I met someone whom I've responded to so right off the bat, so to speak. Tell me, is Bernard sexual, or has he had to renounce such things in order to achieve this remarkable business success?

TOBY: I am not well acquainted with Bernard's sexual habits, dear lady.

(Bernard and McHenry enter from the bedroom carrying a homemade coffin. They cross the stage and exit into the kitchen.)

TOBY: *(Continued. Lowering his voice.)* I, on the other hand, should like to make it known that while I do not possess the spiritual and intellectual vigor of a Bernard, I take a keen interest in sport.

BARBARA: Unfortunately it is not you that I am interested in, dear Toby, though

I can affirm the truism that funerals excite the libido. I have soiled myself twice since my arrival upon the premises.

TOBY: I too have found myself aroused, good lady.

BARBARA: Oh?

TOBY: Your Mr. Sullivan has hardly been safe with me in the kitchen.

BARBARA: Now, that would have been a rare experience for Mr. Sullivan, I can assure you.

(McHenry and Bernard enter with the loaded coffin.)

BARBARA: *(Standing.)* I sense the service is about to begin, Toby.

MCHENRY: He don't weigh but a little bit, sir.

BERNARD: He was a light man, yes.

(They set the coffin down. Barbara peeks inside.)

BARBARA: Oh, isn't he lovely.

BERNARD: And he is the first, Barbara.

MCHENRY: Here's to many more where that come from, sir.

BERNARD: Oh, I foresee an endless supply of death, McHenry. Endless. And I see myself improving at my craft as time goes on, becoming more and more adept at burying selfish desires beneath the needs of the bereaved.

TOBY: A beautiful thought, sir. A beautiful thought.

BERNARD: It's what I feel.

TOBY: And I do not doubt that there is a tidy profit to be gained as well.

BERNARD: There is always that, Toby. But there is more. Much more. In opening our homes to the dead, we open our hearts to death's beauty and mystery. In freeing ourselves from the deadly ministrations of the funeral profession, we free our minds to a fresher, more vivid contemplation of life's final adventure. Let us do for our dead ourselves, I say! Let every home become a funeral home!

BARBARA: Bravo!

TOBY: Hurrah!

BERNARD: May I conclude by saying that I find it fitting indeed that Mr. Sullivan — whose restraint in the matter of popcorn led to a new way of life for others — should be the very one to lead us into what I hope will become a universal practice of home funeraling.

BARBARA: "Let me," he said. "Allow me."

TOBY: Such a splendid little fellow.

MCHENRY: Said the Pope to his Peter. *(Beat.)* Sorry. Sorry, ma'am. *(To Audience.)* Everyone.

BERNARD: Amen.

(Pause, while all silently contemplate the coffin. A knock at the door.)

BERNARD: If you would please, McHenry?

(McHenry opens door. Singer enters.)

SINGER: *(Sings: "Pie Jesu" from Faure's Requiem.)*

END OF PLAY

INVITATION TO A FUNERAL

by Julie McKee

To Lyne and Mike

ORIGINAL PRODUCTION

Invitation to a Funeral was directed by Deborah Hedwall with the following cast:

Shirley . . . . Jayne Haynes
Joyce . . . . Julie McKee

PLAYWRIGHTS BIOGRAPHY

Plays by Julie McKee in the HB series are *Jill On a Recliner, Reading; Haere Mai Ki Aotearoa (Welcome to the Land of the Long White Cloud),* and *The Daffodils,* all published by Smith and Kraus. Other short plays include *A Backward Glance, The "Far-Flung,"* and *A Farewell to Mum* (EST Marathons and published by Smith and Kraus). Recent full-length plays include *Free Ascent, Get It While You Can,* and *The Adventures of Amy Bock* (Yale Repertory Theater, Sundance Playwrights Lab, Yale Summer Cabaret, HB Playwrights Foundation and a finalist in the Chesterfield Writer's Film Project). *A Play by Ear* is to be produced at the HB Playwrights Foundation in its 2001–02 season. Ms. McKee was commissioned by the Ensemble Studio Theatre/Alfred P. Sloan Foundation of Science and Technology Project to write *Fringe Benefits.* She is the recipient of the Truman Capote Fellowship and Eugene O'Neill Scholarship from Yale, and she recently received fellowships from the New York Foundation for the Arts, the MacDowell Colony, and Virginia Center for the Creative Arts. Ms. McKee is a graduate of the Yale School of Drama MFA Playwriting Program (1996).

CHARACTERS

SHIRLEY, late forties–early fifties. Housewife, mother, blue-collar worker. Working class. Bitter, competitive. Rough around the edges. Whatever the departed wants, she wants the opposite. Determined to thwart. Discovers she still has feelings for him.

JOYCE, late forties–early fifties. Housewife, mother, blue-collar worker. Working class. Bright, bubbly, a little naïve, looks on the bright side. Afraid to look death in the face. Discovers she wasn't loved.

NOTE

The audience should not be able to see inside the coffin. It's more fun if the audience watches Shirley's and Joyce's reactions to the "body" in the coffin.

INVITATION TO A FUNERAL

Summer. The present. Lights up in the viewing room of a funeral parlor. Shirley is sitting there alone, in the front row, dressed in black, looking grim. She's about to light a cigarette when Joyce enters dressed in bright colors.

SHIRLEY: *(To herself.)* Oh Christchurch.
JOYCE: *(Loud whisper.)* Is this the viewing room, is it?
SHIRLEY: *(Unfriendly.)* Yeah . . .
(Shirley sits carefully and quietly in the back row.)
JOYCE: Had a look, have you?
SHIRLEY: Yeah.
JOYCE: Look all right does he?
SHIRLEY: Yeah.
JOYCE: Peaceful?
SHIRLEY: Unfortunately.
JOYCE: *(Hopefully.)* Normal, sort of?
SHIRLEY: *(Sharply.)* He's dead!
JOYCE: Oh yes I know. But. Has he got any clothes on? Because he sent me this memo, you know, saying he was going to go out the same way he came in. So I just sort of . . . wondered. *(Beat.)* So. Is he —
SHIRLEY: *(Short.)* Take a look for yourself.
JOYCE: No, no I think I'll wait. Thank you.
(Long pause — Joyce gets out her memo.)
SHIRLEY: *(Begrudging.)* I got the memo too.
JOYCE: Oh did you?
SHIRLEY: Yeah.
JOYCE: So you were married to him too, were you?
SHIRLEY: Oh yeah.
JOYCE: So was I. Don't know quite what he saw in me to tell you the truth.
SHIRLEY: Yeah well. To each his own.
JOYCE: Oh yes. *(Pause.)* Chronologically speaking where are you in the line?
SHIRLEY: I don't know.
JOYCE: Oh. I just wondered, 'cause there's quite a few names on the memo.
(Shirley gets out her memo.)
SHIRLEY: Buncha tarts! At first I thought they was in the order of marriage, what did you call that?
JOYCE: Chronological.

SHIRLEY: Oh right. *(Eyeing her.)* But then I noticed the list was alphabetical. *(Referring to her memo.)* See I'm here, this is me, and I know this one here, see this tart? *(Ominous.)* Bloody bitch of a woman, had a face on her like a run-over beer can, hope she don't show up, I'll bloody smack her one, course she was after me chronologically speaking. And this one over here, she's before me alphabetically speaking, so.

JOYCE: *(Sitting next to Shirley.)* Oh. So you're Shirley!!?

SHIRLEY: Yeah. Who are you?

JOYCE: *(Producing her memo.)* See here. That's me. Joyce. The one *before* you. Chronologically speaking, I think I was, if I remember correctly?

SHIRLEY: *(Eyeing her.)* Oh. *(Begrudgingly.)* Hello Joyce.

JOYCE: Hello Shirley. Didn't recognize you. How are you?

SHIRLEY: I've been better. *(Pause.)* Bugger of a man weren't he?

JOYCE: Oh yes.

SHIRLEY: A real bugger.

JOYCE: Sexy though. I liked having sex with him.

SHIRLEY: Ran off and left me with the kids.

JOYCE: Oh yes, me too!

SHIRLEY: Two sulky, grizzling, bloody kids!

JOYCE: Me too!

SHIRLEY: "Two" must have been the "I better bugger off now" number. *(Pause.)* Left you anything in his will?

JOYCE: Shouldn't think so. Never had a pot to pee in, did he?

SHIRLEY: No.

JOYCE: No.

SHIRLEY: Would have been nice for the kids though.

JOYCE: Mine don't care anymore. Better things to do today, they said.

SHIRLEY: Mine care. All hot to trot. Specially the eldest. She remembers him.

JOYCE: Oh that's a shame.

SHIRLEY: Tough, it's tough. Blames him for her shitty life.

JOYCE: Perhaps he's got some insurance?

SHIRLEY: Life, I should think.

JOYCE: Oh nice. So who's he married to now?

SHIRLEY: Oh some young thing.

JOYCE: Oh no I don't think so. I don't think she'd be young. Oh no. He liked his women mature. Every time he got married they got older. I mean you are older than me aren't you?

(Shirley gives her a look.)

JOYCE: *(Continues. Oblivious.)* So I think the one he's married to now must be old enough to be his mother. I think perhaps that's what he needed all the time, you know, pretty common problem really.

SHIRLEY: Either way she'll get it all.

JOYCE: Stands to reason, yes.

SHIRLEY: Maybe it'll be shared.

JOYCE: He shared everything else, didn't he? Ha, ha, ha.

(Shirley gives her another look — silence.)

SHIRLEY: You going to have a look at him, OR WHAT?!

JOYCE: No. *(Beat.)* Did you remarry?

SHIRLEY: Of course, someone had to give me a hand with the kids, and then I went and had two more.

JOYCE: Oh nice.

SHIRLEY: *(Disgusted.)* God! Weren't much better the second time around.

JOYCE: Pluses and minuses.

SHIRLEY: At least this one stuck around. More's the pity. Grouchy touchy bugger.

JOYCE: Mine's an actual idiot. *(Beat.)* I liked him, over there, best.

SHIRLEY: Me mother couldn't stand his guts.

JOYCE: Good sense of humor though.

SHIRLEY: Only one who could make me laugh.

JOYCE: Full of confidence though, wasn't he? I liked that about him best, 'cause I never had any.

SHIRLEY: Had to slap a writ on the bugger to get me maintenance.

JOYCE: Me too!

SHIRLEY: I'm happy I've outlived him though. Gives me some sense of satisfaction.

JOYCE: Very clean, he was. And very, very particular about his hair.

SHIRLEY: I've actually come to dance on his grave.

JOYCE: Oh well, that's not very nice.

SHIRLEY: I know.

JOYCE: But look at him now.

SHIRLEY: I am. And he's dead. Wearing a flipping cowboy hat.

JOYCE: Oh nice!

SHIRLEY: Holding a joint.

JOYCE: Oh heck!

SHIRLEY: Buck naked. And I haven't had a good laugh since you left, you miserable sod. *(Beat.)* Want me to look with you? I'm ready to have another look. Come on.

JOYCE: No. Yeah. No, no, I can't. I just popped in to pay my respects.

SHIRLEY: Rest assured the hat is very strategically placed.

JOYCE: Is it a big hat? Ha, ha, ha.

(Music suddenly comes on loudly startling them both.)

SHIRLEY: What the hell's that?

JOYCE: What's that?

SHIRLEY: Pink Floyd. 1973.

JOYCE: Oh nice.

(Shirley dances.)

SHIRLEY: Cool. *Dark Side of the Moon.* Remember it?

JOYCE: No.

(The music goes off as suddenly as it came on.)

SHIRLEY: Hey! What the hell's going on? What happened to the music?

JOYCE: Shirley, you know what I think!!? I think it's for the service. I think he'd like for you to be dancing on his grave.

SHIRLEY: *(Immediately alerted.)* What do you mean?

JOYCE: *(Waving the memo.)* He *wants* it to be a party, a big celebration! Look, see, he's having it catered special and everything, lobster sandwiches, an oyster bar, sausage rolls, the lot.

SHIRLEY: *(Defiantly.)* Oh Yeah!? Yeah!? Well in that case I'll just sit myself down.

(She does.)

JOYCE: All my favorites.

SHIRLEY: If he thinks I'm going to enjoy this, he's got another think bloody coming.

JOYCE: After the cremation we're scheduled to scatter his ashes in the ocean.

SHIRLEY: Can't even let me celebrate his funeral without he's running things.

JOYCE: Have you, you know, said good-bye to him?

SHIRLEY: No! But that's besides the point. I didn't come to say good-bye did I? I came to say bugger off and good riddance, and enjoy myself doing it. But if you want to say good-bye you better get in now before those other tarts start lining up, because according to this memo, there's going to be quite a few.

JOYCE: So is he really?

(Shirley nods.)

JOYCE: *(Continues.)* And the hat is?

(Shirley nods.)

JOYCE: *(Continues.)* No, no, no, no, no. *(Laughs nervously.)* Oh. *(Seriously.)* Yeah. All right. You only live once. Okay then.

SHIRLEY: Want me to come with?

JOYCE: Yeah. In case I faint. I might.

(They go up to the coffin.)

JOYCE: *(Continues. Glued.)* Oh.

SHIRLEY: Yeah.

(After a moment or two.)

JOYCE: Weren't no oil painting was he?

(They look for a moment longer before . . .)

SHIRLEY: I'm going to lift up the hat, all right?

JOYCE: *(Horrified.)* No. No. *(Beat.)* All right.

(Shirley lifts the hat.)

JOYCE: *(Continues.)* Oh look, oh. Sweet. Gave me a lot of pleasure that did.

(Silence.)

SHIRLEY: Real carrot top weren't he?

(They look for a few moments. Shirley puts back the hat. They are still for a moment or two before Shirley puts her hand back in the coffin.)

JOYCE: *(Horrified.)* NO! What are you going to? Put it back! Put it —

(Shirley has pulled out the joint.)

SHIRLEY: *(Smelling the rolled joint.)* Oh yeah, yeah, yeah. Best quality. He would have rolled it himself as well. The prick.

JOYCE: *(Staring intently in the coffin.)* You notice anything odd?

SHIRLEY: No.

JOYCE: Something's not quite right.

SHIRLEY: I don't see nothing.

JOYCE: Something's definitely not quite right.

SHIRLEY: I can't tell.

JOYCE: Are you shedding a tear?

SHIRLEY: NO!

(She is. She puts back the joint.)

SHIRLEY: *(Continues. Tearfully.)* He actually called me up before he went, you know, to say good-bye. I hung up on the bugger.

JOYCE: Oh now there, there.

SHIRLEY: *(Fiercely.)* I'm all right. I'm all right! Nothing wrong with me!

(She sits down.)

SHIRLEY: *(Continues.)* It's just that now I'll never know what he wanted to say, that's all. Perhaps he wanted to say he was sorry.

JOYCE: I don't think so, no.

SHIRLEY: How do you know?

JOYCE: 'Cause he rung me up too.

SHIRLEY: What?! The miserable sod.

JOYCE: Said if there's a hereafter, he'd see me there. I said, oh no, I don't think so, because I'm coming back as a dog. Ha, ha, ha, ha.

SHIRLEY: A what?

JOYCE: *(Still laughing.)* I don't know why I said it. Why did I say I was coming back as a dog? *(Beat.)* 'Cause both my dogs had good lives.

(Joyce cries loudly.)

SHIRLEY: Christchurch.

(Shirley gives her a hanky.)

SHIRLEY: *(Continues.)* Hey! He weren't worth it. He left you with two kids to fend for yourself.

JOYCE: *(Snapping.)* Well what are you doing here then!?

SHIRLEY: *(Flustered.)* I come to, to, to — So shut your gob!! *(Beat.)* Oh.

(Leaning over the coffin.)

SHIRLEY: *(Continues.)* Christchurch! Do you see it, do you see it? *(Wondrously. Referring to the part in his hair.)* It's parted on the wrong side.

JOYCE: Oh right.

(They are transfixed.)

JOYCE: *(Continues.)* Do you think we should. You know. Fix it?

SHIRLEY: No. NO!

JOYCE: It looks —

SHIRLEY: *NO!* We'll just sit here, and . . .

(She sits down.)

SHIRLEY: *(Continues.)* And observe. Ha, ha, ha. See if any of those other tarts notice.

JOYCE: *(Horrified.)* It's not funny.

(Shirley checks her makeup.)

SHIRLEY: Cheer up for Christ's sake! How do I look? Do I look all right?

JOYCE: Yeah.

SHIRLEY: You too. *(Beat.)* God I'm dying for a fag.

JOYCE: A dog! What a stupid. *(Then with sad awareness.)* Both my dogs were loved.

(Then Shirley gets out a miniature vodka, hands it to Joyce.)

SHIRLEY: Here.

JOYCE: Ta. Thank you, Shirley.

(Joyce drinks heartily.)

SHIRLEY: Don't mention it, Joyce.

JOYCE: *(Overwhelmed and in tears at Shirley's "kindness.")* That's nice. Isn't that nice? Thank you, thank you so . . .

SHIRLEY: Shut up Joyce! *(Shirley drinks.)* Life goes on. And on.

JOYCE: *(Pulling herself together.)* Think I better study the memo then, take my mind off it.

SHIRLEY: Right!

(Shirley goes up to coffin and retrieves the joint.)

JOYCE: *(Reading the memo.)* Look here Shirl, it says *no black.*

SHIRLEY: I know, but it's me favourite color.

JOYCE: *(Seeing the joint in her hand.)* Oh my.

SHIRLEY: Shame to let it all go up in smoke innit?

(Shirley puts the joint in her mouth and strikes a match. Blackout. In the blackout, the flame flickers for a moment or two, then goes out.)

END OF PLAY

GONE MISSING

by Edward Napier

I'd like to dedicate this play to my great friend, Martha Rollins, who also happened to be my high school speech, art, and drama teacher. Thank you, Mrs. Rollins.

Original Production

Gone Missing was directed by Stephen Dimenna with the following cast:

Lorraine	Amy Wright
Dottie	Annette Hunt
Patty	Abigail Gampel
Katie	Alexandra Napier
Randy	Scott Lebowitz

Playwright's Biography

Ed Napier's first play produced in New York, *Junior Prom,* was directed by the late Herbert Berghof at the HB Playwright's Foundation. His other plays have been seen at such theaters as the WPA, MCC, the West Bank Cafe, Trocadero, the Ensemble Studio Theatre, Nada, Alice's Fourth Floor, P.S. 122, the Salon, the Amateur Comedy Club, and the Workhouse Theatre, where he was playwright-in- residence. A few pieces of his work have been published by Dramatists Play Service and Smith and Kraus. He graduated from Columbia University where he was awarded the Writing Program Award. He received a Berilla Kerr Award for Playwriting and was a Columbia Senior Writing Fellow. He serves on the Columbia University High School Summer Program as a creative writing and performance instructor. He was a guest artist at James Madison University. Currently, Mr. Napier is an adjunct professor of playwriting at NYU and teaches playwriting at HB Studios. He is a member of the HB Playwrights Unit, the Playwright's Coalition at MCC, and the Playwright's and Director's Unit at the Actor's Studio. He studied acting with Herbert Berghof, Sandy Dennis, Yevgheny Laskoi, and Carol Rosenfeld.

GONE MISSING

Lights up on Lorraine, a well-dressed woman in her late thirties looking for something in an open casket — as she continues to look, she grows frantic. She opens the bottom of the casket. Dottie, the sixty-year-old funeral director, enters. She watches her for a moment.

DOTTIE: Honey?

LORRAINE: *(Screams.)* God, you scared me.

DOTTIE: What you lookin' for?

LORRAINE: Where's Mother?

DOTTIE: They're changin' her.

LORRAINE: What? This will be the fifth dress!

DOTTIE: Well, your sister, Kate, poor little old thing, doesn't think your mommy looks as good as she might.

LORRAINE: Well, she's dead! How's she supposed to look?

DOTTIE: Well, now, that's what I taken and think, but now, Lorraine, I am in the funeral business — as you know, and I have come to this: if you take an old woman who was as sick as your mommy for as long, and you can lay her out in a box, so that folks can recognize her when they come to call: Well, you're shootin' par! Let's put her that way ! *(Makes an O with her mouth — something she does when she thinks she's said something clever or insightful. She suddenly changes the subject.)* Hey! Do you play golf up in New York?

LORRAINE: No.

DOTTIE: Isn't that a shame?

LORRAINE: Dottie, I never played golf.

DOTTIE: Well. Good game. *(Sudden shift of thought.)* But you know, I'll just tell ya: Between me and you — her hair could be better. Because I know when she was first diagnosed with the Alzheimer's disease about ten years ago, she taken and told Thelma Mills that she wanted her to do her hair for her funeral, because Thelma fixed her hair — for lo' — almost thirty years — as you know. But now, Thelma, has taken and got the rheumatoid arthiritis so bad, Honey, that she has to drive up to Charleston every month to get the doctor to shoot steroids right into her knuckles! *(Makes O.)*

LORRAINE: Oh my God!

DOTTIE: Ouch! But Honey, even with her steriod treatment, Thelma hasn't fixed your mommy's or anybody's hair for over three years now — it's sad — it really is, but now, given how gone your mommy was these last few years, if Thelma had done it, she wouldn't have knowed it! *(Makes O.).*

LORRAINE: Well, that's a really comforting thought, Dottie. Thank you for that.

DOTTIE: Oh, Honey, you're welcome. Mint?

(Enter Patty, thirty-two, Dottie's daughter.)

PATTY: Mother, we have a flower delivery. Would you please receive it?

DOTTIE: Why don't you receive it!

PATTY: Because I have been on my feet all day, Mother! While you were across the street layin' on your big duff watchin' soap operas. That's why.

DOTTIE: She's the one who did your Mommy's hair. *(Makes O.)*

LORRAINE: It looks very nice.

PATTY: Thank you.

DOTTIE: Of course, I don't think so.

PATTY: Why, Mother, I cut my own hair.

DOTTIE: And you can tell it, too! *(Makes an O.)* She was too good, Lorraine, to go to mortician school over in St. Louis like her brother. She had to go up to West Virginia and study political science, but she never did anything with it though!

PATTY: Mother! Go get the flowers! Just go! Go, go, go, go, go, go, go!

DOTTIE: Don't you speak to me that way.

(Dottie exits.)

PATTY: I swear to God! Sometimes, I'd like to just wire her mouth shut! I mean, Mother was always a talker — as you know.

LORRAINE: Oh, I know.

PATTY: But since she has started taking Prozac, she just will not shut up! *(Makes an O with her mouth.)* But listen, Buddy, she needed it. In a period of two months her mom died, our rat terrier, Suzanne Summers, died, my dad died, and my brother came out! And he was married with a kid and was forty years old. I mean: *(Makes an O with her mouth.).*

LORRAINE: Your brother, Steve?

PATTY: *(Giggles, stops.)* I always knew it. We're both gay. Anyway. It was like too much of a convergence — of events? So after about three months of her being a total lunatic, I'm like "Mother, you have to get a grip. You must go to therapy. I mean, people aren't stigmatized on account of it anymore, because so many people go see a psychiatrist on TV!" And she was like, okay. And now, she's doin' a lot better. She really is.

(Enter Katie, thirty, angry.)

LORRAINE: Good. Excuse me, Katie, where's Mother?

KATIE: I don't know.

LORRAINE: You don't know where Mother is.

KATIE: Oh. Mother's downstairs in the embalming room. I thought you were asking me about that fucking ring again!

LORRAINE: Well, I can't find it anywhere!

KATIE: I cannot begin to tell you how offensive I find your insinuating that I stole Mother's ring.

LORRAINE: Well, someone had to have stolen it.

KATIE: Well, I didn't steal it!

LORRAINE: Patty, have you seen Mother's diamond cluster? It's gone missing.

PATTY: You mean, the ring that you all decided to bury her in?

LORRAINE: Yes. Because Katie decided that the engagement ring Dad gave her should be mine. Grandmother's engagement ring is hers. And Mother's cluster: she's getting buried with.

KATIE: That way, we each get one — one diamond ring. I think, that's fair. Do you think that's fair, Patty?

PATTY: Well, I reckon.

LORRAINE: Well, I'll tell you one thing: The viewing begins in an hour, so I'm putting my foot down about the dress! We're not changing Mother's dress again, today.

KATIE: Well, we'll just have to see. Depends on how she looks.

LORRAINE: You've been changing Mother's dress all afternoon, Katie. She's not a Barbie doll. Jesus!

KATIE: Hey, fuck you, Lorraine.

LORRAINE: No, fuck you, Katie!

PATTY: Well, I always like to see you Thacker girls together — I tell you. It's just like old home week. You know?

KATIE: And fuck you, too, Patty!

PATTY: Well, Katie, what'd I do?

KATIE: You did the worst dye job on Mother's hair! And you did it to be spiteful. You did it to be mean.

PATTY: I did not!

KATIE: I beat you out of the trombone section's first chair in high school, and you just never got over it.

PATTY: Shit, that was almost twenty years ago. Paranoid.

LORRAINE: And I think Mother's hair looks pretty.

KATIE: *(Beat.)* It's purple!

LORRAINE: It's always been purple.

KATIE: Not that purple! And that's why I can't find a dress to put her in — her hair clashes with everything. *(Cries.)*

LORRAINE: She looked pretty in that green silk dress I bought her in London.

KATIE: She did not! She looked like a great big Easter egg.

(Dottie enters with flowers.)

DOTTIE: 'Lo! Aren't these flowers pretty though? These are the teacher's sorority, and these are from the Kenova Chapter of the Order of the Eastern Star. Uh-oh!

(As Dottie places flowers. Randy enters.)

DOTTIE: *(Turning toward the door and sounding like a banshee.)* NO, RANDY! NO! NO! NO! YOU GET YOURSELF OUT THAT DOOR, NOW! OR I'LL TAKE MY FLY SWATTER TO YOU! NOW, I MEAN IT! GO ON! GET!

LORRAINE: Who was that?

DOTTIE: Juanita and Oley Crabtrees' Mongolian idiot boy, Randy. He comes over here all the time to steal flowers, and bless his heart, he'll take 'em over to his mother, and sometimes, she brings 'em back, but sometimes, she doesn't, and that's not nice. But I try to teach him — which is why I am stern with him — treat him like a dog. And he loves me.

LORRAINE: *(Examines flowers.)* Did the obituary not say, instead of flowers, the family requests donations be sent to the Alzheimer's Foundation in Mother's name?

KATIE: That is so typical of you.

LORRAINE: What?

KATIE: Mother would of liked the flowers, Lorraine! She liked flowers. She liked to garden. She was on the town beautification committee for half of her life! Is that something you learned at Smith, or from your rich husband? No flowers — just money for a foundation.

LORRAINE: No.

KATIE: I won't ever forget that nightgown — that Christian Dior nightgown you sent to Mother when you couldn't come help me move her from our house to the nursing home — after Mother stopped being able to distinguish between the toilet and — everything else. And you were so critical of that. Tried to make me feel awful about it. Yet you hardly ever came down here to see her. Brought her only granddaughter to visit her once — one time.

LORRAINE: Mother didn't even register the fact that she'd met Gabriella.

KATIE: She knew more than you gave her credit for, Lorraine. Every day after school — I'd go see her. Last August, she started thinking I was you. I guess, I liked it. She was so proud of you.

LORRAINE: I loved my mother. I wanted to come to visit her more often.

KATIE: But you didn't. And now, you come down here, and you write an obituary that discourages people from sending flowers and hire a Presbyterian minister to say the eulogy.

LORRAINE: He's supposed to be very good.

KATIE: MOTHER WAS CHURCH OF CHRIST!

LORRAINE: STOP SCREAMING AT ME! I'm sorry. I mean, I know you are upset, Kate. But honest to God, Mother had Alzheimer's disease for eleven years, were you not at all emotionally prepared for this death?

KATIE: No.

PATTY: *(Quietly to Katie.)* Mint?

LORRAINE: And since I got here, you have done nothing to help make the proper arrangements! And I had to find a minister, an organist, write the obituary, prepare a lunch at the Women's Club after the burial tomorrow, choose a coffin, a vault — while you lay downstairs in that basement apartment Mother made you — that lair of yours smoking marijuana! And listening to Joni Mitchell! I mean, the whole idea that you are the high school guidance counselor is slightly — horrific!

KATIE: Well, usually, I am more functional, but whenever I see you, I have this — I don't know — this weird kind of regression. I think, it has something to do with the way you smell.

LORRAINE: What?

KATIE: That perfume.

LORRAINE: My perfume? What? "Je Reviens"?

PATTY: I think Lorraine smells good. *(Sniffs the air.)* But hey, speaking of vaults: I have your all's vault certificate for you — in this drawer over here.

DOTTIE: No, God, don't do that!

PATTY: Yes, Mother, Clark Grave Vaults wants all their customers to have the thousand-year guarantee certificate.

DOTTIE: No!

PATTY: Yes, Mother. What is your problem? Get a grip! It's procedural.

(Patty opens the table drawer.)

PATTY: Mother, might this be the diamond cluster in question?

DOTTIE: Well, I had to get your all's attention one way or another. Didn't I?

PATTY: Well, Mother, I believe, you certainly have it. *(Makes O.).*

DOTTIE: I think, you girls are awfully ugly to one another. And I know, that is just the last thing your mommy would want. She'd want you to be kind — to everybody, but especially to each other. When your dad left, you all were just little bitty girls, and I know, she just loved you — more than anything. Because that's how all mothers feel about their babies — no matter what anybody says.

PATTY: You love me that much, Mom!

DOTTIE: Yes! *(Beat.)* Except when I hate you, I do. *(Makes an O.)* But you know, girls, the Egyptians buried folks with jewelry and stuff, but your mommy — well, we as Christians believe: that that traveller ain't here. A precious ring is a thing for the living — what memory it might evoke. Old dead body ought to just rot.

LORRAINE: Well, what are we gonna do about the ring, Katie? It was your idea to bury Mother with it.

KATIE: She bought that cluster for herself. She wore it all the time. It was her ring.

LORRAINE: I know, it was. And that is why when you suggested that we bury her in it, I said, fine. If that's what you want, fine.

KATIE: *(Beat.)* Well, I think, we should give it to Gabriella. When she and Peter get here for the funeral — tomorrow.

LORRAINE: To Gabriella . . .

DOTTIE: I think your mother would want her granddaughter to have her ring. That's proper.

LORRAINE: *(Beat.)* You know, I used to call Mother on the phone — all the time — when I was at Smith, and when I first moved to New York, and I'd say, Ma, I want to come home, and she'd always say, "You sound like a hillbilly. Don't be hillbilly." And I always wanted to say — but — but I didn't — I am. (I am).

(A voiceover through Dottie's walkie-talkie.)

VOICEOVER: Hey, Mom? Mrs. Thacker is ready to go, again.

DOTTIE: Okay, Steve, Honey, I'll be right down to take a quick look.

(Dottie crosses to the coffin and opens the bottom section of the lid.)

DOTTIE: We need some more butter mints in that candy dish. You've been eatin' 'em all afternoon. And every five is a hundred calories.

PATTY: Mother, shut-up.

DOTTIE: Don't you tell me to shut up! I'm your mother!

(Dottie and Patty exit.)

LORRAINE: Why don't you give Gabriella the ring? I can't believe all these people are going to be descending on us in a few minutes. Do I look all right?

KATIE: You look fine.

LORRAINE: Katie, I know, you probably think this is shallow; but I haven't seen some of these people in thirty years! And I care about my appearance! I just do.

KATIE: You need lipstick.

LORRAINE: Thank you.

KATIE: How about me?

LORRAINE: Brush your hair!

(Lorraine applies makeup. Katie brushes her hair. Randy enters. Steals the flowers and exits. Lights fade.)

END OF PLAY

THE DIVINE CHILD

by Lisa-Maria Radano

To my kid, with apologies

Original Production

Girl . . . . Molly Carden
Old Woman . . . . Carla Briscow
Woman . . . . Caren Browning

Playwright's Biography

Lisa-Maria Radano has worked in film, television, and theater. Film work includes *Mrs. Winterbourne, Velocity,* and *Kingdom of Frank.* Television work includes "The Tracey Ullman Show." Her first full-length play was produced and directed by James L. Brooks in Los Angeles. She was also a recipient of a New York State Council for the Arts Grant. She lives in Greenwich Village with her husband and daughter.

THE DIVINE CHILD

An Old Woman sits on a sofa in a funeral waiting room. Enter a Woman and a Girl. The Woman cries throughout.

GIRL: Ma?

WOMAN: Oh my God — I can't — I tried but I can't —

GIRL: Mom?

WOMAN: I mean, Christ — I'm sorry but, I'm just not good at this —

GIRL: Mommy?

WOMAN: — to be alive one moment and then — so — so —

GIRL: Ma!

WOMAN: — so what. What is it. What.

GIRL: Can I have a quarter?

WOMAN: No. What for.

GIRL: There's a candy machine in the pee pee room.

WOMAN: Candy? Don't talk to me about candy. This is not a day for candy! *(Fresh tears. The Girl turns away, downhearted.)*

OLD WOMAN: *(Thick Italian accent.)* Pardon me. I sorry to intrude inna you but, do you care for perhaps a nice tissue?

GIRL: Tissue? I don't even know you!

OLD WOMAN: Che?

WOMAN: That's her favorite joke.

OLD WOMAN: Choke? *(Confused.)* I sorry I no speaking so well —

WOMAN: No, no, it's her. She didn't tell it right. You're supposed to do it when somebody *asks* for a tissue. Go on, ask me for a tissue.

OLD WOMAN: I gotta one. You want?

WOMAN: No *ask* me.

OLD WOMAN: Hokay hokay. Can I have a tissue?

WOMAN: Tissue, I barely know you! Get it? Tissue? You get it??

OLD WOMAN: Still no.

GIRL: Tish — you. TISH. YOU? Get it??

WOMAN: Don't mind her. It's a stupid joke.

GIRL: Well I like it! Jesus fucking Christ! You never let me have anything I like! I can't even have candy! I'm a kid! I need candy!

WOMAN: Those aren't candies in the toilet, all right? Those are breath mints! People like to have fresh breath at a fu — fu — *(New tears.)*

GIRL: Mom . . . C'mon, Ma.

(More tears.)

GIRL: Oh forget it.

(The Girl throws up her hands. The Old Woman hands the Woman a tissue, turns to the Girl.)

OLD WOMAN: Littla girl. Whassa you name?

GIRL: Smegma.

OLD WOMAN: Smegma? *(To the Mother.)* What kinda name eesa thees?

(The Woman waves her away, crying on.)

OLD WOMAN: Hokay, Smegma. You wanna these advice from a very old woman?

GIRL: Not particularly.

OLD WOMAN: *(Cheerfully.)* Hokay. Be nice to you mama, I'ma thinka she vady oo-set.

GIRL: Upset.

OLD WOMAN: Dass it. Oopset. She vady oop-set.

GIRL: Well this is not exactly an Elizabeth Arden jour the beaut-ay for me either!

WOMAN: *(To Old Woman.)* Please — just ignore her.

GIRL: That's right. Just ignore me! That's your specialty!

WOMAN: Shut up okay? Just shut up! Shut up shut up shut up!

OLD WOMAN: Hokay use two. Basta. You both sit beside to me onna the cooch. You both lean onto me, onna the cooch. Is nice my arms is nice anna fat. Come.

GIRL: I'd rather suck gas. *(Girl stalks off to a chair.)*

WOMAN: Well *I'll* sit next to you. And aren't you kind to offer. *(She sits, dabs her eyes, leans a bit.)*

WOMAN: *(Continues.)* There. Sitting. Better. Your arm *is* nice and — and —

OLD WOMAN: Fat. Is good. Va bene.

WOMAN: — I guess I really am as you say, oop-set. I mean, I hate to sound self-absorbed —

(The Girl snorts.)

WOMAN: *(Continues.)* — but a death in the family gets me thinking about *my* life.

OLD WOMAN: I'ma check-a the pantry.

WOMAN: Right. Like, have I lived the way *I* wanted? Do *I* have any reasons to be proud of my life?

GIRL: I'll go look for some but I may need a few weeks and a truffle pig.

(The Woman throws herself against the Old Woman and wails.)

OLD WOMAN: Basta, Smegma, shh —

WOMAN: Don't shh her, she's right! My life is just this great big puddle with a used Band-Aid floating in it!

OLD WOMAN: Ay — I try to help done make-a me sick —

WOMAN: I'm sorry. I just have not been very happy. Do you understand? I have never been very happy.,

OLD WOMAN: Si si. Per che, cara?

WOMAN: When I was about her age some people that were kind of key, died.

OLD WOMAN: Who.

WOMAN: My parents!

OLD WOMAN: Madonna.

WOMAN: I know. They were lost at sea —

OLD WOMAN: Swimming?

WOMAN: No no, they were flying to Block Island on a small plane and we don't — we never —

OLD WOMAN: Aspeta aspeta. A smalla — che?

WOMAN: A small plane. You know? Plane?

(She puts her arms out like wings.)

OLD WOMAN: *(Suddenly irate.)* Che cazzo succede a la gente? Non hanno mai sentito di Buddy Holly?

WOMAN: Take it easy.

OLD WOMAN: — *Tutti devono una gran maledetta fretta! Cosa che di cosi importante per dover correre supito supito supito — per che??? Per poi finire come Patsy Cline? Big Bopper?? Per quanto io vivro non potro mai capire! Basta cosi! Take-a da mothera fuckena BUS!*

GIRL: Whoa. Mama Leone's got a temper.

OLD WOMAN: Okay, cara. Talk talk. You saying someteens about you so wretch and depressa you whole life.

WOMAN: Well, I've had some good moments here and there. Chiefly on vacations.

OLD WOMAN: No no. You miserable. We know.

WOMAN: Well really — the depression was never serious — it was more like a dial tone or a jackhammer down the block that you just get used to — you know? You entrain it. You make lunch, you make braids, you make plans. You give. But then one day, you realize that nobody is looking at you anymore. Not even construction workers. I mean shit — the same guys whose screams heralded my budding adolescence, now can't even be bothered to look up from their baloney sandwiches! My youth was like a gorgeous little puppy I tied up outside the supermarket, not knowing I'd be gone twenty years, and when I finally came back out, all that was left was a rusted leash and a few dry bones.

OLD WOMAN: Is notta too late for you cara.

WOMAN: Oh come on! It's over for me! I've turned into one of those women in rubber-sole shoes, with a WNET tote bag, picking over the fruit at Fairway — just another invisible old HAG! — Oh God, I'm sorry, I —

OLD WOMAN: No no, cara, va bene, I like to be hag. I like this for me.

WOMAN: Well I don't. I used to like being looked at when I took a stroll.

GIRL: I told you — wear a hat! A bright and colorful hat! She never listens to me!

WOMAN: What's the point? I was born old. The universe conspired to rob me of my youth.

GIRL: So you decided to do the same thing to me.

WOMAN: That's not true! Is it?

GIRL: Take a look at how you dressed me today.

WOMAN: It's a funeral!

GIRL: I know that you've got me dressed up like a stockbroker! I'm a kid! I should be wearing little —

OLD WOMAN: Toe shoes.

GIRL: Right, and sequins and feather boas!

WOMAN: Don't be ridiculous.

GIRL: I'm a fucking child, it's my fucking job to be ridiculous! Ahhhh!!!

(She throws herself onto a floor.)

OLD WOMAN: *(Sharply.)* Smegma, you get up anna talk nice to you mama —

WOMAN: Stop calling her Smegma, she happens to be right! I have been totally unfair to her! And who the hell are you anyway? Have we met? You remind me of someone . . .

OLD WOMAN: Cara — go to her. *(Reaches in her purse.)* Give her this one —

(The Old Woman brings out an enormous multicolored lollipop.)

WOMAN: I don't allow sugar.

OLD WOMAN: Give her.

WOMAN: Okay, okay.

(The Woman reluctantly takes the lollipop, crosses to the Girl.)

WOMAN: *(Continues.)* Hon? It's me. I came to say I'm sorry.

GIRL: *(Head buried.)* For what.

WOMAN: For being a lousy mom.

GIRL: You're not a lousy mom. You're an amazing mom.

(Then.)

Just not to me . . .

OLD WOMAN: *(Whispers.)* Give her the pop.

WOMAN: C'mon kid, gimme a break, I said I was sorry.

GIRL: You don't even know what you're sorry for! All I ever wanted was for you to hold my hand and take me places. Act proud of me. Buy me a little dress with a pattern. Listen to me once in a while. I had such good things to give you. Things so they never would have looked away from you. Nobody. Ever. To overlook you.

OLD WOMAN: Give her the pop.

WOMAN: You know, I feel like I know your voice.

OLD WOMAN: The pop, the pop, give her the pop!

WOMAN: Hon, I have something for you. Look at me.

(The girl looks up. The Woman lets out a sharp gasp of pain.)

GIRL: What — you told me to.

WOMAN: I know — it's just — your face is so beautiful. Here —

(She holds out the pop.)

GIRL: Wow! You never let me have candy!

(She throws her arms around the Woman.)

WOMAN: Does this mean you forgive me?

GIRL: Sure.

WOMAN: Just like that?

(The Girl plops into the Mother's lap, unwraps the pop.)

GIRL: Just like that.

WOMAN: You're going to open that now? *(Off Girl's look.)* Sorry, sorry.

(They embrace, holding one another close.)

WOMAN: Okay, that thing is getting in my hair.

(They continue to embrace as now — a handsome young Mortician enters, moving a partition to reveal a coffin.)

MORTICIAN: Ladies?

OLD WOMAN: Ahh! Fucken guy scared the crap outa me.

MORTICIAN: The service is about to begin. Shall we?

WOMAN: Not her — she's too young to —

GIRL: I'm cool. Got my pop.

WOMAN: But — you can't have that in the —

GIRL: Sure I can. Right?

(She nods.)

OLD WOMAN: Hokay ragazzi, we go.

(They rise. The Woman turns, sees coffin —)

WOMAN: Oh God —

GIRL: What now?

WOMAN: Oh Christ —

GIRL: It's just a coffin.

WOMAN: I know what it is! Who picked it out? It's hideous!

MORTICIAN: Ladies?

WOMAN: No wait, lipstick —

GIRL: It's on.

WOMAN: Husband —

MORTICIAN: He's here.

(Woman pats her body.)

WOMAN: Babies! Where are my babies? Three human beings passed through this body to get here —

(They all lead her.)

WOMAN: *(Continues.)* — I gave birth! I baked a hundred and fifty-two birthday cakes! I did my best! I hate funerals! I hate suffering! I need more time! I need more — *(Standing behind coffin.)* — Jesus fucking Christ, will you look at this thing? I mean what was he thinking?

OLD WOMAN: He wuzza no think he wuzz cry. Cry.

WOMAN: You know I really hate to be rude but what are you doing here?

OLD WOMAN: I you. We alla bitsa you.

WOMAN: *(Can't understand accent.)* What?

GIRL: I'm your Divine Child, and Granny here's the wise old woman who lives in your head.

WOMAN: Wait a second. You're my wisdom?

OLD WOMAN: Dass it.

WOMAN: But you don't speak English!

OLD WOMAN: No no. I'm Italian.

WOMAN: But I'm not!

GIRL: Ma . . .

WOMAN: *(To Mortician.)* Can you believe this? Me and my wisdom had a fucking language barrier! Did God feel the need to give me additional challenges??

GIRL: C'mon, Mom. Don't stall, it's so loser-y.

WOMAN: I am a loser. I wasted my life.

MORTICIAN: Honey, look. You loved. You were loved. Okay, so you didn't exactly vault a ten. You still got here. And anyway I like you. You're funny.

(An organ starts playing dismal chords.)

WOMAN: Really? Well you — you're very cute for a — *(Then.)* Wait a second what is this, I specifically asked not to have goddamn —

(He raises a hand — the music becomes "Whiter Shade of Pale.")

WOMAN: *(Continues.)* — organ music, I — oh — I love this song. I had my first kiss to this song. It was in Steve Lambert's basement. He had the most amazing sound system . . .

(He kisses her. She melts. A tear runs down her cheek.)

WOMAN: *(Continues.)* Do you have a tissue?

GIRL: Tissue? I barely know you.

(The Old Woman chuckles.)

OLD WOMAN: I get it! I get it! *(And so on . . .)*

(The woman enters the coffin with the help of the Mortician.)

WOMAN: Well. All things considered I'd rather be back in the basement. But thank you. For reminding me.

(The Mortician exits. The Old Woman looks on as the Girl lovingly hands the Woman the pop. Finally, the Woman rests in peace. And the Girl and the Old Woman can now exit into the ether as we fade to black.)

END OF PLAY

THE FUNERAL PLAY

by Theresa Rebeck

ORIGINAL PRODUCTION

The Funeral Home was directed by Max Mayer; production stage manager was Richard Hodge with the following cast:

Jim . . . . Joe Urla
Roy . . . . Gerard O'Brien

PLAYWRIGHT'S BIOGRAPHY

Theresa Rebeck's plays include *Spike Heels, Loose Knit,* and *The Family of Mann* at Second Stage; *View of the Dome* at New York Theatre workshop and Victory Gardens, *Sunday on the Rocks* and *Abstract Expression* at the Longwharf, and *Dollhouse* at Hartford Stage. Other productions include New Georges, The Workhouse InTenCities project, EST, the Westbank Cafe, New York Stage and Film, Actor's Theatre of Louisville, the Source, Alice's Fourth Floor, Manhattan Punchline, Double Image Theatre, Naked Angels, Theatre Geo, Seattle Rep, HB Playwrights Theatre, and the International Women in Theatre Festival. She received an NEA grant for her continuing work on the musical adaptation of the nineteenth century melodrama *The Two Orphans.* A collection of one-acts, *Rebeck Revisited,* ran for nine months at Theatre Neo in L.A., making the L.A. weeklies' ten best list as one of the ten best plays of 1999. Ms. Rebeck's plays have been published by Samuel French as well as Smith and Kraus, who, in addition to publishing her collected plays, have included her work in the *Women Playwrights: The Best Plays* annual series five times. *The Butterfly Collection* was workshopped at South Coast Rep and New York Stage and Film, summer 2000, and produced at Playwrights Horizons in the fall of 2000. Ms. Rebeck is a member of Naked Angels, New York Theatre Workshops' Usual Suspects, and HB Playwrights lab. She has enjoyed residencies at ACT/Hedgebrook and the New Harmony Project, where she workshopped her play, *The Bells.* New plays also include *Omnium Gatherum* (co-written with Alexandra Gersten) and *Bad Dates.* She is currently working on commissions for South Coast Rep and City Theatre in Pittsburgh.

In television, Ms. Rebeck has written for the HBO series "Dream On," "Brooklyn Bridge," "LA Law," "Maximum Bob," "First Wave," "Third Watch," and "NYPD Blue," where she also worked as a producer. She is currently consulting producer on "Law and Order: Criminal Intent." In film, she has written and produced *Kalamazoo,* an independent short starring Wallace Shawn and Adrienne Shelley. Produced features include *Harriet the Spy* and *Gossip.* She wrote *Catwoman* for di Novi Pictures/Warner Brothers, *The Richest Girl in the World* for 20th Century Fox/RKO Pictures, and *War Crimes* for Francis Ford Coppola and is currently writing *Bloodlines* for Irwin Winkler.

Awards include the Mystery Writer's of America's Edgar Award, the Writer's Guild of America award for Episodic Drama, the Hispanic Images Imagen Award, and the Peabody, all for her work on "NYPD Blue."

Ms. Rebeck earned her MFA in Dramatic Writing and her Ph.D. in Victorian Literature at Brandeis University, where she met her husband, the stage manager Jess Lynn. They have a seven-year-old son, Cooper.

THE FUNERAL PLAY

Roy is sitting alone next to the coffin, grieving quietly. Jim enters, cautious. He considers him for a long moment, not sure about interrupting. Finally, he clears his throat. Roy looks up, startled.

JIM: Hi. Hello. *(Beat.)* I'm sorry for your loss.

(Roy nods, goes back to his meditation. Jim tries to think about how to begin again.)

JIM: *(Continuing.)* When is the service? This afternoon? The service is this afternoon?

ROY: People will be visiting, in, half an hour. I was hoping to just have a few minutes alone with her before people started to arrive.

(Having gently made his suggestion, Roy tries to meditate some more. Jim shifts on his feet, awkward.)

JIM: Oh of course. Absolutely. *(Checking the coffin.)* Your mother, huh? I mean, you've, uh, lost your mother, I guess.

ROY: Yes.

JIM: That's a hard thing. To lose a parent. To lose your mother. Unless you weren't close. Of course sometimes that makes it worse. I mean some people think I feel okay about it, but that's not normal or healthy or . . . sorry. *(Beat.)* You don't remember me, do you?

ROY: No.

JIM: That's okay. I mean, I don't blame you, you're going through a very hard, very stressful, I mean — well, how could you remember someone you met sort of in passing, not passing exactly, but . . . anyway.

ROY: Listen. I don't mean to be rude.

JIM: You really don't remember? The Imperial Rest versus the Eternal Slumber? The Nocturnal Peace?

ROY: *(Recognizing him.)* Oh.

JIM: Yeah.

ROY: How are you?

JIM: Okay. So it worked out? The . . .

(He points to the coffin.)

ROY: Yes. Thank you.

(He touches the coffin, reverent.)

JIM: Good, good. That's what I . . . I just wanted to make sure.

(Beat.)

Because there was a little confusion, actually. Downstairs. When they were, actually I'm not even sure where the confusion, but you know, there was so much you had to deal with, I'm sure, the flowers and the guest list, open or shut, which, you know, which coffin. A lot of questions during what is unquestionably a very, very sad time.

ROY: Look, is there something you . . . need?

JIM: No no. I just, because of the confusion. There are a lot of funerals that happen right on top of each other, back to back, well, that's not the right, anyway, people die, and everyone, sometimes many funerals happen at the same time, and there are several bodies to be prepared downstairs, and the coffins line up, they, there are often several, in a row, downstairs. I'm sure you can imagine how that would happen.

(Roy looks in the coffin, worried, then looks at Jim.)

ROY: *(Defensive.)* That *is* my mother.

JIM: Yes. Yes, oh, I didn't mean to imply otherwise. It is. It's just not . . . her coffin.

(Roy looks at him, uncomprehending.)

JIM: *(Continuing.)* You know, we had the conversation? Imperial Rest, with the satin lining and the brass fixtures, not to mention the goosedown, that's, it runs several thousand more than the Eternal Slumber, not to mention the more, um, economical but perfectly, perfectly reasonable, fine, Nocturnal — you know, the Nocturnal —

ROY: Peace.

JIM: Exactly so.

(There is a pause. Jim is very unhappy. Roy looks at the coffin.)

ROY: We're very happy with our selection, is that what you're asking?

JIM: Yes, I guess so. *(Beat.)* Because it's not actually, you see, your selection. You paid for, that is, you selected the Nocturnal Peace, and somehow, well, frankly, through my — confusion — or, some might say, error — your mother was placed in the Imperial Rest, which was actually paid for by Mr. and Mrs. James Riordan, of Canarsie, for her grandmother may she rest, you know, in et cetera.

(He is silent. Roy considers this.)

ROY: So this isn't my, my mother's coffin, that's what you're saying.

JIM: Unfortunately no.

ROY: So what are you, what are we supposed to — people are coming. People are arriving, my father and his — all their friends not to mention siblings and — people are coming to mourn, to mourn her.

JIM: Absolutely, absolutely.

ROY: I mean what are you saying, that we're expected — because of your screw-up, this is a terrible thing for our family. She was a deeply loved woman, we all are in real —

JIM: I hear you —

ROY: And you want what? What is it you want, for us to move her body into a different coffin because of your mistake? I don't care about your mistakes now! My mother is dead, and the people who loved her are gathering, today, now, gathering to —

JIM: No no, I totally —

ROY: This is not my problem! Now, would you please get out of here so I can spend a few — my mother is dead, you asshole.

JIM: I see. Okay. You're completely right. I just wanted to mention it.

ROY: Well, you did. And I intend, this is completely unacceptable. At a time like this to be asked — I intend to let people know I find this completely unacceptable.

(He sits, puts his hand on the coffin, protective. Jim nods, miserable.)

JIM: Of course. I'm sorry. I didn't mean to disturb you.

ROY: Well, you did. You are! Why are you still here, will you just please leave me in peace, in some small amount of peace before I have to put my mother in the ground? What is — I am going to report you. I, understand me, I will have your job over this.

(Beat. Jim thinks about what to say to this. Roy sits, angry, by the coffin, waiting for him to leave.)

JIM: Well.

ROY: Well, what? Well why are you still here? How many times do I have to ask you to just get the hell out of here?

JIM: You know, you — I know you're upset, but you shouldn't be mean. I'm upset too, all right? I mean, there's no point in your threatening to, to have me *fired.* I've already been — it was on the outside chance, I mean, that I *could* maybe get my job *back,* that is why I came here, to see, to see if at this terrible time in your life you might have a little, maybe, com*pas*sion for a fellow traveler, that was the reason I thought to speak to you.

ROY: If you don't get out of here now, I will call your ex-boss and have you thrown out. Christ.

JIM: *(Angry.)* Listen — hey — listen — ask yourself, you just need to ask yourself then, if I came here and told you that you got a cheaper coffin, than than than the one you paid for, if you would think it was such a crazy idea, that you should switch the coffins. You ask yourself that. I mean, you act all outraged, but you wouldn't think it was so *nuts* if the whole money thing went in the other direction.

ROY: *(Enraged.)* What?

JIM: I mean, I lost my job over this, I — and my mother's dead, too, you know. She died, it wasn't that long ago, I feel your pain. My mother died, I was the only one there, my stupid sister is in *Baltimore,* and she can't be bothered, my father is at home in a wheelchair and I can't call him, from the hospital and tell him, so much was happening so fast, and besides which they didn't know, they didn't see it coming although she did. She did, and I — so many things just happening at once, and the doctors, no one will tell you — meanwhile, my sister the IDIOT cannot be reached, they want to know about putting Mom on machines, which she did not want, it was so clear, she signed a *document,* and when I call Dad he just breaks down and wants to come down to the hospital but he's home alone, and I can't, she's going, I wasn't, to leave her? How could I? Because I was — to have to say good-bye so quickly — I'm sorry, but — to have to say good-bye so quickly to someone — I mean, I was there, and for that I am grateful, for all of it, the confusion, and the horror, not being able to, to say what — I am grateful. To have been there. And I did, I did close her eyes. Which was very, very hard, but I wanted to do it for her. Because I loved her very much. And then of course there was hell to pay. My father, why I didn't have them turn those machines on so that he would have time to come down there, his *anger* — which probably was just his grief redirected, although frankly you do get tired of having every one of his vast array of emotions redirected into anger so that he can dump it right on you — whatever. Whatever. And then there's my sister, who breezes into town after all of it and just takes over. Which coffin, what kind of flowers, what readings at the service, Bach and Schubert for the processional, she's just on top of everything and I am no longer, believe me, so the funeral is absolutely perfect and there's nothing of my mother in it. Nothing at all. And they're both so angry with me, for the way I — but I couldn't do it, I just couldn't. Put her on those machines just for them. It would have been wrong. And now of course they will both, yes, of course I have lost another job, well, I don't know why I took it any way, to take a job in a funeral home three months after your mother dies, that's just crazy, unless it's just so you can keep, keep . . . *(Beat.)* Sorry. Really, I'm sorry. I just, uh, I do feel your pain, and I know you want to be with your mother today. To have this time. I know that. I envy you that. *(Beat.)* I do, I envy you that.

(Beat.)

ROY: Look. Do you want to sit down?

JIM: No, no, I —

ROY: No, really. You want to take a few minutes?

JIM: I . . .

ROY: It's okay. Really. Go ahead. Here.

(He gestures toward his seat, next to the coffin.)

JIM: Oh.

ROY: Please. She would like that. She would.

(He gestures again. Jim goes to the seat, sits. Roy stands to one side of him. After a moment, Jim reaches out and touches the coffin. He takes a minute. Roy bows his head, steps over, and touches the coffin as well. As the two men say good-bye to their mothers, fade to black.)

END OF PLAY

DOTTIE AND RICHIE

by Jacquelyn Reingold

This play is for Scott

ORIGINAL PRODUCTION

Dottie & Richie was directed by Susann Brinkley

Richie . . . . Mark Nelson
Dottie . . . . Geneva Carr

PLAYWRIGHT'S BIOGRAPHY

Jacquelyn Reingold's plays, which include *Girl Gone, Dear Kenneth Blake, Dottie and Richie, Tunnel of Love, Lost and Found, A.M.L., Joe and Stew,* and *Freeze Tag,* have been produced in New York at the MCC Theatre, Ensemble Studio Theatre, Naked Angels, HB Playwrights Theatre, All Seasons, Working Theatre, Circle Rep Lab, and at theaters across the country and in London. Her play *Acapulco,* recently published by Smith and Kraus, received New Dramatists' Whitfield Cook Award for best unproduced play and has had readings and workshops at Naked Angels, HB, the Atlantic Theatre, and the ASK Theatre Projects. Ms. Reingold's other awards include New Dramatists' 2000 Joe Callaway Award, a commission from EST/Sloan Foundation for her new play *String Fever,* the Kennedy Center's Fund for New American Plays' Roger Stevens Award, and two Drama-Logue Awards and she was a finalist for the Susan Smith Blackburn Prize. Her work has been published by Dramatists Play Service, Samuel French, in *Best American Short Plays 1999–2000, 1997–98, 1996–97* and *1994–95, Women Playwrights: The Best Plays of 1994,* and in *New Dramatists: Best Plays of the Graduating Class 2000.* Her screenplay adaptation of *Girl Gone* has been optioned by Beech Hill Films, and she has written for MTV's *Daria.* Ms. Reingold is a recent alumnus of New Dramatists and a member of Ensemble Studio Theatre. She has written many plays for the 52nd Street Project.

CHARACTERS

RICHIE, forty. A nice Jewish comedian from Brooklyn. A sweet man with a big heart. He talks quickly, using his hands. Nice on the outside and on the inside. And not to be underestimated.

DOTTIE, thirty-five. Conflicted and confused. With an edge. Trying to do the right thing. For the first time. Feels like she's nice on the outside, but Medusa on the inside.

PLACE

Riverside Memorial Chapel on the Upper West Side of Manhattan.

TIME

December 6, 1999.

DOTTIE AND RICHIE

Richie and Dottie in a room in a funeral parlor. He wears a suit. She is in work-out wear.

RICHIE: *(In midstream.)* And it was crowded I mean just people everywhere: Ed Koch, Joan Rivers, Regis, his wife Joy, Al D'Amato, Claudia Cohen, the gossip columnist he went out with, Dr. Judy Kuriansky, a pop psychologist who's been married about twelve times, Joe Franklin. No room downstairs at all, so I got in the elevator and there's Danny Aiello, and Steve Grouper, who has this cable-access show where people call him up and insult him and that's the whole show, and then I realize I'm standing next to, believe it or not, Imelda Marcos.

DOTTIE: Did you look at her shoes?

RICHIE: No, I didn't even think to, and she was the only one allowed off at the mezzanine, the rest of us weren't, even Jerry Stiller and Anne Meara, who I said hello to 'cause I know them 'cause I met them in East Hampton when I did a comedy festival that they saw and he came up to me afterwards, he thought I was good and asked me to write something for his roast — did you see it? — so I did. Anyway, he used a sentence of mine, which was nice, and Anne Meara who I had previously met two years ago when she said a very strange thing to me, anyway the rest of us, including Joy Behar, got off at the third floor after Imelda was gone, and I'm usually not so pushy but I managed to get my way onto the balcony and stood right next to Caroline Hirsh who owns Caroline's, Abe Beame, and Peter Max, I think it was Peter Max, and I had a perfect view.

DOTTIE: Good.

RICHIE: And people spoke, and kept referring to the mayor and the first lady, and I thought it was Hillary, but I guess it was just Donna, and the mayor got up and made this awful joke about how he tried to take a cab over, but no one would stop and pick him up. And uh Cindy, Joey's wife, said something about Sirio letting them have a good table at Le Cirque even during Joey's last days when he wasn't eating well. I guess that's her idea of a great act of humanitarianism. And the rabbi, of course, and then some kind of minister who said, "The last time I saw Joey, he was in a wheelchair and when I asked him if he was comfortable he said . . . 'I make a living.' " Which was funny, old but funny, and then he said it a second time, which wasn't so funny.

DOTTIE: Uh huh.

RICHIE: I just felt it was important for me to be here. To pay my respects. I mean Joey was a friar, I'm a friar, he was a comic, I'm a comic. And he had me on his radio show once. In the eighties.

DOTTIE: Uh huh.

RICHIE: I haven't been to a funeral since Mr. Henny Youngman passed. And it struck me, how death is the big equalizer, you know? I mean, Imelda Marcos, Michael Musto, Mathilda Cuomo, and me, all here on December 6, 1999. To mark the death of Joey Adams.

DOTTIE: Yeah?

RICHIE: And then I thought of you. And last night. I couldn't stop thinking about you. Seeing you. How amazing it was. And I remembered I left my wallet. At your place. So right after the service ended, I called. And here you are. Thanks for coming by.

DOTTIE: Sure.

RICHIE: I would have been happy to come over.

DOTTIE: This place is a block from my gym. And I was about to go work out.

RICHIE: You look beautiful.

DOTTIE: I didn't even shower.

RICHIE: You not showering is beautiful.

DOTTIE: You're sweet.

RICHIE: No, you are.

DOTTIE: You're very sweet.

RICHIE: I had a great time.

DOTTIE: Yeah?

RICHIE: I've never — I mean — I don't know how to say this — I've never had a night like that, I never felt that, and I've been with other women and. I have no words. For me, that's something. I even lost my appetite. I was hungry and we still, and then we ate — after. I'm just so happy to see you.

DOTTIE: Yeah?

RICHIE: Maybe we could go for a bite to eat? Now that I have my wallet back. Maybe a tuna sandwich, a nice pasta, or a salad, something light. I know you like to eat light. I'd like to like to eat light. I mean I know I had a steak last night, with french fries and blue-cheese dressing. And cake. But I could eat light. Like Thai or Italian or.

DOTTIE: Look.

RICHIE: I am. I could look at you a lot. I could look at you today, I could look at you tomorrow. Oh, tomorrow. I'm doing a benefit, with Professor Irwin

Corey at the Jewish Home for the Aged on the West Side, maybe I could come over after. I know it's more than a block away, but it is on the West Side, and you're on the West Side. And next week I'm hosting a singles variety show at the Y. I could interview you.

DOTTIE: I wouldn't know what to say.

RICHIE: I'm sure they'd love to just look at you, Dottie.

DOTTIE: Richie?

RICHIE: Dottie.

DOTTIE: Richie.

RICHIE: I just want to touch you and smother you with kisses and be with you and spend all day together and all night and all day and —

DOTTIE: I'm not really that great.

RICHIE: Oh, you are.

DOTTIE: No, I, I have bad feet. They get tired, and I have to sit down a lot.

RICHIE: I love to sit.

DOTTIE: And my apartment —

RICHIE: — A palace.

DOTTIE: I don't shave my legs.

RICHIE: I couldn't tell.

DOTTIE: Or under my arms.

RICHIE: I noticed a lovely fuzz.

DOTTIE: And the way I have to, you know, in order to —

RICHIE: — It's my pleasure to serve.

DOTTIE: I'm still stuck on my ex.

RICHIE: I can handle that.

DOTTIE: I have overwhelming feelings of rage towards any man I'm with.

RICHIE: Who said life was easy?

DOTTIE: Bad relationship history, you know, psychotics, addicts, pathological liars. The terminally ill.

RICHIE: Then perhaps you're ready for a change.

DOTTIE: I've been considering becoming a lesbian.

RICHIE: I'd love to hear all about it.

DOTTIE: Allergic to pets.

RICHIE: Maybe a nice poodle, hair not fur, you know?

DOTTIE: A polyp in my uterus.

RICHIE: I'll be there for the surgery. Dottie, you bring out the best in me.

DOTTIE: Richie, how is it you're still single?

RICHIE: 'Cause I never met a girl like you. You're who I always dreamed of, but never knew. 'Til last night. *(He touches her.)* I wish this were a nice bed and breakfast and we could go upstairs, order in, and then I'd kiss you. *(He kisses her.)* And touch you. *(He touches her.)* And take off your clothes. *(He's all over her.)*

DOTTIE: *(She pulls away.)* I killed Joey Adams.

RICHIE: Excuse me?

DOTTIE: I killed him.

RICHIE: What do you mean?

DOTTIE: It was me.

RICHIE: You are speaking I take it, in a metaphorical type of way.

DOTTIE: I am not who you think I am. As wonderful as last night was, that's how awful it will get.

RICHIE: And uh the fact that he was eighty-eight years old and had cancer, this had nothing to do with how he died?

DOTTIE: There are lots of ways it can happen.

RICHIE: What exactly is going on here?

DOTTIE: I am not your dream girl. In fact I'm your worst nightmare. I don't even look like this. This is just me in the beginning. When the trap is being set. Then, maybe it'll be an accident. A burn from coffee that's too hot, a depression that leads to suicide. Stand-up comic slips on a banana peel and falls to his demise. Funnyboy, don't let me touch your funny-bone again. 'Cause you'll be crying your way back here from the inside of your very own box. You get where I'm coming from, you keep away or you'll go the way of Joey Deadman Not Walking Adams. He's greeting the grubs and meeting the maggots, no more "Just for Laughs" for him. I saw his last act, and he didn't kill. I did. So be a stand-up guy and open your eyes, 'cause I'm coming your way. Plane crash? It's probably me. Arson? I've arrived. Succubus? I'm by your side. So, nice man, Mr. Comedian, who likes to make 'em laugh, you with the stars in your eyes and the swell in your pants, run away I say, before it's too late. And I throw my long locks over the side of the castle, then take off my wig and watch you tumble down to Hell.

RICHIE: I appreciate you have some uh intimacy issues.

DOTTIE: Intimacy?

RICHIE: I was thinking if maybe we could just let things develop, you know in a natural way.

DOTTIE: Natural, what's natural? Look around, what do you see? The leftovers, the skins, the once-wet now-dried formaldehydes of those that dared to love me.

RICHIE: You wanna get something to eat and talk about this?

DOTTIE: I will devour you for breakfast and spit you out at lunch.

RICHIE: You did say you were in therapy, right? Is it once a week or twice?

DOTTIE: Fool. I am warning you to get your clown feet in highest gear and get the hell out of here.

(He steps away. Then comes back.)

RICHIE: Why are you telling me this?

DOTTIE: Don't look a gift horse in the mouth.

RICHIE: If it were true, why would you say?

DOTTIE: No reason.

RICHIE: Nonsense . . . I'm not going anywhere until you answer.

DOTTIE: A warning, okay?

RICHIE: But why?

DOTTIE: 'Cause you're sweet.

RICHIE: What do you know from sweet except it tastes good? You liked me.

DOTTIE: I like no man.

RICHIE: It was different this time.

DOTTIE: It's always different: car crash, cancer, broken bungee cord. I don't get bored.

RICHIE: Admit it. You liked me.

DOTTIE: I felt pity.

RICHIE: A monster like you?

DOTTIE: Skip the flattery.

RICHIE: You like me.

DOTTIE: An absurdity.

RICHIE: I win.

DOTTIE: Excuse me?

RICHIE: You may have killed Joey Adams, but I am Joey Adams. And all those that came before him. And I'm still here. It didn't work, see? I'm still listening. I'm still breathing. I'm still making jokes. I'm not riddled with bullets. I am the riddle. I keep coming back. Ice me, and I melt. Kill me, and I laugh. Your fatal bite gives me delight. Your venom tastes like nectar. You're not so bad.

DOTTIE: I lure them in like honey, then watch them drop like flies.

RICHIE: Well, I'm not much of an insect myself.

DOTTIE: You will regret this day.

RICHIE: I know what I felt.

DOTTIE: You felt what I wanted you to feel.

RICHIE: I saw it in your face.

DOTTIE: You saw what you wanted to see.

RICHIE: You think I'm stupid? You think I'm weak? You think I don't know what I'm doing? I beat you at your own game. You softened. Under my breath. I was there.

DOTTIE: Nonsense.

RICHIE: You warned me. You warned me. You care. I could see it in your eyes, I could taste it on your lips. It's been an eternity. But I win. You're mine. I'm yours. The end.

DOTTIE: It was just a ploy.

RICHIE: You took off your own peel, and you slipped, sweetie. You made a mistake.

DOTTIE: You didn't realize.

RICHIE: *You* didn't realize.

DOTTIE: You made a mistake.

RICHIE: It's over.

DOTTIE: No, it's not.

RICHIE: You're right. It's just beginning.

DOTTIE: No, it's not. It's over.

RICHIE: Then why don't you just walk away?

DOTTIE: You.

RICHIE: You.

DOTTIE: You.

RICHIE: You.

DOTTIE: *You.*

RICHIE: *You.*

DOTTIE: You.

RICHIE: You.

DOTTIE: You.

RICHIE: You.

(They lean in to kiss. They quickly pull away. They lean in to kiss. They stop abruptly, lips almost touching. Blackout.)

END OF PLAY

MATHEMATICS

by Daniel Reitz

To Mark, Rose, and Megan

Original Production

Mathematics was directed by Peter Wallace with the following cast:

Camon . . . . Todd Alan Crain
Dennis . . . . Jonathan Woodward

Playwright's Biography

Daniel Reitz's plays have been developed and produced at numerous theaters, including the Mark Taper Forum, the Joseph Papp Public Theater, Naked Angels, Manhattan Class Company, Playwrights Horizons, Ensemble Studio Theatre, and Circle Repertory. He was a recipient of a 2000 fellowship from the New York Foundation for the Arts, a Drama-Logue Award, and *L.A. Weekly* Theater Critics and Ovation Award nominations. For his play *Where I Come From,* he was a finalist for the Heidemann Award at the Actors Theatre of Louisville's Humana Festival. He has also received writing fellowships from the Edward Albee Foundation, the MacDowell Colony, the Virginia Center for the Creative Arts, the Yaddo Corporation, and the Hawthornden Castle International Retreat for Writers in Scotland.

Urbania, his screenplay adaptation of his play *Urban Folk Tales,* was voted Best Film at film festivals in Los Angeles, San Francisco, Philadelphia, and Provincetown, was nominated for a Grand Jury Prize at the Sundance Film Festival, and was an official selection of the Toronto and Seattle film festivals before its release by Lions Gate Films in 2000. The film also received a GLAAD Media Award nomination. He adapted his play *Regular Joe* as a short film and wrote and directed the short *Height of Cool,* both of which have been screened at several film festivals in the United States and Europe.

As an occasional journalist, he has written for the *New York Times* and *Salon.*

Characters

CAMON, forties.
DENNIS, fifteen.

Place

A funeral home in Bay Ridge, Brooklyn. Evening. Spring.

MATHEMATICS

An open coffin, containing a body. Camon, a strikingly handsome priest, enters dressed in black pants, black shirt, white collar. He takes a long look at the body in the coffin and smiles.

CAMON: So handsome dead.

(Dennis sits up, laughing.)

CAMON: Hello.

DENNIS: *(Indicating coffin.)* I could do with one of these bitches.

CAMON: What would you do with it?

DENNIS: Keep it in my room, man. Take naps. Sit like this . . . *(Dennis props himself up with the head cushion.)* Chips here. Bong. Watch TV. Have a brew. *(Opens the other half of the coffin with his foot.)* Keep an ice chest in this part. *(Brings the lid down with his foot.)* How the fuck did ya get us in here, anyway?

CAMON: I'm a priest, that gives me carte blanche access to solemn operations all over town. Tomorrow night I'm scheduled for a wake. I like to check the room beforehand.

(Dennis stands up in the coffin. He wears a basketball jersey, baggy pants, Fila sneakers.)

DENNIS: This is some gnarly shit.

CAMON: I thought you'd enjoy it.

DENNIS: *(Looks around.)* This is where they had my ol' man laid out.

CAMON: Is it? How old were you?

DENNIS: What do you care? *(Grins.)* Never been in one of these fuckin' things before.

CAMON: Never fucked in one before either, I'll bet.

DENNIS: *(Shakes his head, stepping out of the coffin.)* Disgusting. Goddamn *priest.* What a nauseating, you oughta be taken out —

CAMON: And what, Dennis?

DENNIS: Makes me wanna like . . . *puke.*

CAMON: *That,* from the likes of a little Bay Ridge vandal with extreme psychological problems.

DENNIS: Extreme psychological . . . shit. That's a hot one.

CAMON: Is it a hot one?

DENNIS: It sure is. It's a hot one coming from you. You call yourself a priest? You oughta be locked up.

CAMON: Well. That's one theory. *(He produces a videotape.)* This, however, might disprove *that* for some. If this got out. Which it absolutely could. You had the *nerve* . . . in your own parish, your mother's, *mine,* the most treasured statue of the Virgin Mother Ascending, gift of the Veterans of Foreign Wars, imported from Dresden, destroyed by you . . . your semen dripping off her porcelain . . . vile. *(Shakes the videotape, smiling.)* You. Your face. Your little dick. Clever of me to place that hidden camera where I did, wasn't it? How hard would it be, I wonder, to connect you to all those other atrocities, desecrations, defecations . . . carving swastikas on the foreheads of stone angels on children's graves . . . *(Pause.)* By the way, I should tell you . . . it's a hundred thousand dollars now. The reward.

DENNIS: Hundred thousand bucks? Jesus fuck . . . I AM THE SHIT!

(He prances around, rapping from Eminem's "Real Slim Shady.")

CAMON: *(Smiles.)* No, not bad at all. Personally, I thought seventy-five thousand was insulting. It was the Mother of God who brought you into six figures.

(Dennis begins undressing matter-of-factly, kicking off his sneakers, tossing his white socks in the direction of Camon.)

CAMON: What exactly are you doing?

(Dennis shucks off his shirt and socks, throwing them in Camon's direction.)

DENNIS: What does it look like? I'm gettin' the job done here. You think I'd even be here if you didn't call my *house* . . . *(He plays with the zipper of his pants.)* Lookin' for me, tellin' me you wanted to *talk* to me. You don't think my devoted mother noticed that? Not that I give a shit, fuckin' *bitch* . . .

CAMON: Ah, yes. You and your mother . . . and your grandmother, she still lives upstairs, doesn't she? A house of women and you. If they saw your little performance here . . . it would . . . well. They're so . . . *Catholic.* They'd blame themselves. No strong male authority figure.

DENNIS: Let's get this over with.

CAMON: What makes you think this is what I want? Or all I want? My problem is . . . I have such a weakness for the worthless. I guess I always have.

DENNIS: Worthless? With a hundred g's on my head? What are you worth?

CAMON: *(Smiles.)* Let me tell you something. I know your mother. I know all the mothers, the daughters, all the women. They are the lifeblood of any church, of any faith, for that matter. And I see them look at me. *Stare.* You see, the longer you look the more stunning I become, which makes listening to a sensitive homily or a tender eulogy from me all the more compelling. Physical beauty, intellect, and compassion . . . that's the kind of Holy Trinity people can comprehend. Not to mention the little details — what slays them — the subtlest whiff of aftershave, a musky trace on the skin of a devastating-looking man of God, whose life has already been claimed.

(Pause. Dennis pulls down his pants.)

DENNIS: Look . . . you wanna fuck or not?

(Camon laughs.)

DENNIS: Who you laughin' at? *(Pause.)* Fine. Fuck you. I'm outta here.

(Dennis pulls up his pants, picks up the rest of his clothes, dresses.)

CAMON: You think I really won't turn you in? In case you haven't formulated the thought: I now own your ass, you little whore.

DENNIS: *(Smirks.)* You *own* me?

(Dennis spits on the lid of the coffin. Pause.)

CAMON: Tch tch tch . . . would you do that on your mother's coffin?

DENNIS: You turn me in then you won't own my ass anymore.

CAMON: No. But everybody else will. And they won't look like me. You would be my gift to them. As for that hundred thousand in reward money, I'd just give it to charity. Like the good priest I am. I could have a trust set up, put some aside for your rehabilitation. When you're released.

(Camon takes Dennis's hand, pulling him toward the coffin. As they climb in, Camon undoes his own pants and tries to force Dennis's head down onto his crotch. Dennis resists, jerking his head up, and pulls away, stumbling out of the coffin. He struggles to his feet.)

DENNIS: *Fuck you, man! (Pause.)* 'Cause there has to be a reason, right? For doing what I did? I mean, I could say I was pounded by my old man or groped by Father Whatever when I was an innocent little boy . . . I could remember details, sure . . . I could, Holy Fuck, I can *feel* all the memories coming back. Good Friday, 1997. Just before three o'clock mass. The hour of Christ's death. I was eleven. Father — . . . blocked the name out but they could find out . . . called me in early to light the candles. I came in. He was holding the pole that had the gas flame, he had this funny look on his face, he was all sweaty, he said, it's out, you let it burn out, the gas was on, now it's all gone, this thing is worthless. You're worthless. He said, I hate carelessness. You see this thing? This is used up. This is good for nothing. Do you want me to show you what this *is* good for? He showed me. Oh *yeah. (Pause.)* Memories like that. Poor Mom. And Father Whatever, there'd be an investigation, probably. But I'm not using that as an excuse. Except there's always a reason, right? God forgives, that's the beauty of Him, of you, of this, me, you, us, and you're right here to forgive me, and make sure they all follow your example. You got to. You're *required* to. You have to plead my sad sad case and make sure I get mercy. Just a buncha statues after all. Not people. Not little boys.

CAMON: *Feces* on the grave marker of an *Auschwitz* survi —

DENNIS: Doesn't matter. *Because I am now turning myself in to you.* Mercy, mercy. All must be forgiven. You know why? Because I'm a victim, too. It's my story. Look at the way I turned out. Always a reason. It's fucking mathematical.

(Dennis climbs on top of the coffin. He stands on it, looking down at Camon.)

CAMON: Fucking . . . *mathematical* . . . the degenerate's regeneration.

(Camon laughs.)

DENNIS: You think you own me? Look at me. *(Pause.) Look* at me, you . . . *fuck.* Close your eyes. I wanna see how *you* look dead.

(Pause. Camon closes his eyes.)

DENNIS: *(Smiles.)* See . . . *that* gets me hard.

(Dennis feels himself through his pants. Camon opens his eyes, looking up at Dennis. They stare at each other. Blackout.)

END OF PLAY

JEFFREY SLUGWORTH: EX-EMBALMER

by Ari Roth

Original Production

Jeffrey Slugworth: Ex-Embalmer originally appeared in the 2000 HB Playwrights Foundation Funeral Play Festival; directed by Jim Milton with the following cast:

Jeff . . . . Tony Martinez

Playwright's Biography

Ari Roth is the author of *Born Guilty,* based on the book of interviews by Peter Sichrovsky, originally commissioned and produced by Arena Stage, off-Broadway at the American Jewish Theater, and over thirty other productions across the country. Most recently, it was produced in repertory with its sequel, *Peter and the Wolf,* commissioned by the National Foundation for Jewish Culture (NFJC). *Goodnight Irene* was commissioned by Manhattan Theatre Club with a grant from the NFJC and has been produced at the Performance Network in Ann Arbor, Hypothetical Theatre Company in New York, and at Theater J in Washington, D.C., where Mr. Roth serves as artistic director. His play *Life in Refusal,* produced at Theater J in 2000, was nominated for a Charles MacArthur/Helen Hayes Award for Outstanding New Play (as was *Born Guilty* in 1992). His comedy, *Oh, The Innocents,* won the Clifford Davy Award for its production at GeVa Theater, directed by Joe Mantello. It was subsequently produced at HB Playwrights Foundation, directed by Artistic Director William Carden. *Love and Yearning in the Not-For-Profits and Other Marital Distractions* premiered at Theater J in spring 2001 and was originally workshopped at the Ojai Playwrights Conference. The play is expanded from one-acts originally produced at HB Playwrights Foundation. Mr. Roth is a recipient of a National Endowment for the Arts Workshop Grant nominated by Northlight Theatre and has had his one-acts produced at Ensemble Studio Theater, Circle Rep, and the Double Image Short Play Festival. He is a graduate of the University of Michigan where he won two Hopwood Awards for playwriting, and has taught at the University of Michigan, Brandeis, and New York University.

JEFFREY SLUGWORTH: EX-EMBALMER

The basement of Donnelly's Funeral Home. It is empty, dark. We hear the fumbling of keys. A man enters. An overhead lamp is illuminated. Jeff, gangly and awkward, takes stock of the surroundings; the room is gutted.

JEFF: I wasn't expecting to get in. I thought I could do this from the parking lot. You know. Explain? But first off, there *is* no explanation; not for what I did; and second, the sign, out front? "For Sale" — Which makes the saying good-bye all the more difficult; especially if you missed the funeral, which I'm sorry about, Mr. Donnelly. A funeral home director deserves a proper farewell and my face would have disrupted — I know it would've — Looking the way it did.

Drinking can do that. And I'm ashamed that I was. I'm only sorry I didn't know about the illness. The paper said "a long battle"; with something. I couldda helped, had I known. Probably not. Probably best to keep me out of the picture; which I was doing. You probably didn't realize. Which is too bad. Because this is something I really needed to do!

(Recovers.)

Or I'm supposed to — Part of my program. A step — I forget which — There's *so fucking many.* I've done like eight. Or four. One a year; that's about my speed. My favorite: "I am taking my sins out from under the rocks and apologizing to those I have harmed." You can see why it takes some folks as long as it does. A lotta rocks. See, but the accident? It was *just* an accident, and then things became undone and I could not still the tremor and I vowed I would not return until I could. See?

(Holds out his hand.)

Faint. But it's there. I can still it with a tumbler of bourbon. Not advisable for a professional in our line. Plus the face.

It can look like a Frankenstein sometimes. Or a Slugworth. Physiognomy is generally something I have the power to change. With a smile. But if I don't do my upkeep, or forget to shave, or clip, mine's the kind of face you'd see on *Creature Features* Friday nights on channel 9 where the monster comes back holding daffodils — I always liked that, because in life, there's usually a house with a real monster whose face might get bigger and bigger until the membranes burst, and then things start to break, like dishes, or picture frames, and the instruments come out; things like scalpels, or kitchen spoons, or the Marine belt, or sometimes he'd just use his bare hand with the brass ring. And then Mother would run off and he would run after, and I would clean up the vomit, and the glass, and they would come back, one at a time. Which is why I'm such a horror film buff now. Because in real life, Frankenstein never ever returned with flowers.

I'm in maintenance now. Part of my re-hab. I like to make myself useful. To Church groups. Community theaters. Places that need me. This place could need me.

I could buy it back. I've inherited a large chunk of estate — The Old Monster's — So a purchase is not out of the question. I could wear a suit. Same one when you needed me to fill in on the Wurlitzer. Still fits, I would imagine. I've only gotten thinner. I'd like to have something to celebrate. I'm mostly dealing with health issues these days, which is how I know about "long battles." And I could hire an assistant. To do the intakes. I'd stick to what I know and what I know is cosmetology; structural restoration; reordering fluids. It's just a question of recertification. If I can get the nerves steady. Without assistance. Because I'd want to come clean before the licensing board. I'm committed to that.

"What are your strengths and weaknesses?" Well, sutures are my strength, I think you would vouch for that. You taught me the worm stitch; figure eight; double intradermal. And my weak spot, most definitely: Skull jobs. Cranial reconstruction. Someone loses an ear, you're supposed to make one out of putty.

I think that's what stumped me the last time. It was a skull job. That's what I'd tell 'em. We'll be "Donnelly's Funeral Parlor, Incorporated, and We Don't Do Skulls." We'll have a sign. "Natural Causes Only." And we'll include sexually transmitted diseases, because they're natural, and we accept all God's creations. "Just No Accidents."

See, I hit someone. Did I mention? I was going eighty in a twenty on a fifth of Jack and I hit a powder-blue Colt, and they were gonna come back to get me. That's what they said. The police. And I was supposed to wait. In the hospital. That's where they brought me. I don't know what happened to her. Never really found out. That's what I tell people. In meetings. They'll ask if I ever think about the person. But if they were really listening, they'd know I was lying. See? How do I know it was a "her"? 'Cause you generally can't see who you're hitting when you're going eighty in a twenty. "Fifteen when the lights are flashing." That's what the sign said. Guess where I was heading? AA! Pretty ironic, huh? I would speed through this one particular school zone; I'd see the sign — "Caution" — And my instinctive reaction was to floor it, right down to the roadbed. Generally, no one would see me. The young teacher in the powder-blue Colt; she didn't see me. Not till the very last second, and then she couldn't take her eyes off. She had one of those evergreen air-fresheners, and a strawberry birthmark, and the evergreen jerked forward, and then back. I made an effort. I think the record will indicate that I swerved. But there was traffic. And so I veered, avoiding the hydrant but hitting the curb and careening, instead, into the driver's side door, and I went flying and the world went quiet except for the birds and the trees, the approaching ambulance.

And what I remember is a grass embankment of Kentucky bluegrass and then 5:09 in the morning on the hospital clock and figuring I had a very limited window — people would be coming — so I got up, made my way down the hall, and walked the two-and-a-half hours down Chain Bridge Road until I reached the oasis and went to work in the basement, where I was supposed to be.

I scrubbed up; checked the clipboard; opened the fridge to figure out what I'd be working on, and then I saw: Skull job. Ear work required. Full-scale cranial reconstruction — well, not full. The forehead was intact. A female forehead. With a strawberry . . . I stepped back, as you taught me; collected my wits. I did not succumb. I would restore this young woman and deliver comfort and make her whole. And so I reach for my forceps. I'm holding stay clamps. Pick up the metal swab. I'm holding blush. All hand-eye coordination is apparently deserting. I open my hands; hold them up to my face. And I can feel it ripple through my entire body. A tremor. A drinker's tremor amplified by a magnitude so "off-the-Richter" it shook the very foundations and, in truth, has never stopped. Although I try to, from time to time, through a variety of means.

I tried that day. I walked upstairs. I knocked. I didn't wait — I was lucky to get my hand on the knob — And then the family — The family you were meeting with — They took one look at me — And here was the mistake — What I said before, about upkeep; and not doing my hygiene, especially when you're in scrubs and it hasn't gone well and it shows, and there's cuts from the windshield, and a bandage, and they shrieked, and I went running just as fast as I could, which wasn't very, because I was broken; truly; in every imaginable way; and I knew it was gonna take a very long time to get better, and it has.

That's what I'd tell the licensing board. And I'm sure they'd look at me and say, "Well, that's good. That's good, Jeffrey. But not good enough." And I'd agree. And let it go. The dream. I hope that's okay. I think I should not attempt to provide comfort, or solace, or anything close to anyone on a permanent basis for as long as I'm here. Which won't be forever. None of us are.

I only wish we could have talked. That day, I mean. You would have said — I know you would have, "Jeffrey" — you would have said, "We cannot undo death. We cannot reverse the past. The embalmer provides an illusion; of comfort, and in so doing, provides real solace to all bereaved."

I wish I could have provided for you, Mr. Donnelly. What you provided me. But I'm just gonna let it go.

Oh. And . . . here's the key. I was keeping it all this time. Just in case. I ever managed to make it back.

I made it back.

(Looks around.)

Still an oasis.

(Leaves key on table. Exits. Fade.)

END OF PLAY

MILTON BRADLEY

by Peter Sagal

ORIGINAL PRODUCTION

Milton Bradley was directed by Susan Einhorn with the following cast:

Allen . . . . Stephen Singer
Mark . . . . Mark Zeisler

MILTON BRADLEY

A funeral home sitting room. Mark sits in a chair, wearing a dark suit. Late twenties. Allen enters, mid-thirties, wearing a yarmulke and a serious suit.

ALLEN: Mr. Sapstein? Hello. I'm Rabbi —

MARK: Rabbi.

ALLEN: Schoenberg . . . hello.

MARK: Hello.

ALLEN: I'm terribly sorry for your —

MARK: Yes, yes.

ALLEN: Loss.

(Pause.)

MARK: These things happen.

ALLEN: Yes, they do.

MARK: This must be fairly routine for you, I guess.

ALLEN: You know, it never is. Although it's a sadly large part of my job. Any day you start thinking, oh, just another funeral, well, then you come in and see the bereaved, and you realize —

MARK: "The Bereaved."

ALLEN: Yes . . .

(Pause.)

MARK: Did you have to learn this stuff? In rabbi school?

ALLEN: I'm sorry?

MARK: I mean, did they give you a course in like, Talking to the Sad?

ALLEN: No. We just sort of learn as we go.

MARK: How about talking in general? Because I've noticed that a lot of rabbis talk the same, they've kind of got this slow talking thing, "To-day-ay . . . we rea-ad from the Buh-ook of Le-vi-ti-cus . . . " Is there like a course in that?

ALLEN: No.

MARK: Oh. Because I figured there had to be some reason.

(Pause.)

ALLEN: Mr. Sapstein, do you attend a synagogue? Because it was my understanding —

MARK: Oh, no.

ALLEN: That you didn't have a rabbi who knew —

MARK: No, I haven't been inside a temple in years.

(Pause.)

ALLEN: I understand that your mother has been a regular at our services.

MARK: It was sort of an old-age thing. I think she liked to dress up.

ALLEN: It's true, a lot of the older congregants enjoy the social aspect, they're less mobile, you know. Some place to go.

MARK: Sure.

(Pause.)

ALLEN: I never met her. I think by the time I arrived at the synagogue, her illness had progressed to the point where —

MARK: Oh, no, She was fine.

ALLEN: She was?

MARK: Pretty much until the moment she dropped dead.

ALLEN: Well. That's a blessing, really, to avoid a long —

MARK: She hated you.

ALLEN: Oh.

MARK: Not you, really. She never met you. The idea of you.

(Pause.)

ALLEN: Which idea, exactly?

MARK: Who knows. You're too young, too liberal, too smart. You give out page numbers.

ALLEN: Page numbers.

MARK: You know. "Please turn to page 83 of the prayer book." That sort of thing.

ALLEN: Yes.

MARK: She thought if you're too dumb to know which page you're on, you shouldn't be there. So she stopped going. Don't take it too bad. She hated everyone.

ALLEN: Mr. Sapstein. I was wondering . . . as you know . . . I was asked to conduct the service. Which I am glad to do, for anyone, especially a member — a past member of my congregation, even if . . . well, anyone. And I promise: no page numbers. Heh. And it is traditional to mention some qualities of the deceased, so as to appropriately memorialize her. But since I didn't get the chance to meet your mother, I was wondering perhaps if you could tell me some things you would like me to mention. Things you would like people to be thinking about at this moment.

MARK: Oh. Sure. *(Pause.)* She was . . . the biggest bitch you ever saw. A mean vicious old woman. Even before she was old. Still mean. Drove my father to the grave with her hateful, mean ways. She hated everyone who was more attractive, or nicer, or more well liked than she was, which was everyone. She was vain, and a manipulator, and a hypochondriac, which come to think of it was probably just another way to manipulate people. So you don't have to add that. Anytime she saw you taking pleasure in something, some small thing, she'd ruin it. When I was a kid, I had a skateboard. Just a skateboard. Used to ride it down the street. She destroyed it with a sledgehammer. No. I take that back. She made me destroy it, with a sledgehammer.

When we were small children, she used to punish us for no reason. She'd never hit us or anything, she'd just let us know that she was angry. Her favorite thing was to start crying: big fat tears. "You hurt Mommy's feelings! Go to your room!" And we'd go to our room, because what the hell did we know. I remember once, I must of been six, and I finally said, "What did I do, Mommy?" And she said, "If you have to ask, you don't really love Mommy."

Everything we ever did, or tried to do, she told us it wasn't a smart idea, or wouldn't work. You know the nonsense things that kids do, the drawings of, like, little houses and horsies and stuff, and every mother in America would pin them up and be so proud? She would always say the same thing: "What is that." Not "What is that?" like expressing some enthusiasm and wonder, but "what *is* that." Like she knew, she knew, and we hadn't figured it out yet. Oh, we did though. It was sufficient.

You know, I look back now, I figure what she was trying to do? I think she was trying to wreck us, so she could look at our awful lives, and say, see? I told you you'd never amount to anything.

(Long pause.)

ALLEN: Did she . . . have any enthusiasms? Hobbies?

MARK: Gossip. Spreading rumors. Tearing down people behind their backs. Like you. She said —

ALLEN: How about friends?

MARK: I don't think they liked her either. She had a couple of old ladies she talked about, but mainly just to make herself feel big. Whenever she told stories about them, it was about how stupid they were and how she had to set them straight. I think some of them are going to be here, just to gloat.

ALLEN: Mr. Sapstein. It's none of my business, but it seems there are a lot of unresolved feelings here —

MARK: They're resolved now.

ALLEN: Still.

MARK: I mean, she's dead. Doesn't that pretty much wrap things up?

ALLEN: You'd be surprised.

MARK: I'm always amused by this idea that every person is, like, essentially good. Just confused or angry or misunderstood. I think some people are stone evil, personally. They just take their pleasure from other people's pain.

ALLEN: I don't think you're right.

MARK: That's because you didn't know my mother until after she was dead. She's harmless, now.

(Pause.)

ALLEN: I understand how you must be feeling. But in about five minutes, I am required — it is my job — to stand in front of your mother's coffin. Is there anything you'd like me to say, or do, besides stomping on it?

MARK: I just told you.

ALLEN: You mean . . .

MARK: That's what she was like.

ALLEN: But . . .

MARK: You want to spare everybody's feelings? Why? She'd *want* them to feel uncomfortable. She'd want them to look at the floor and wish they were anywhere else. That's what I did, my whole life. Why change now?

ALLEN: There must have been some good thing. Some accomplishment.

MARK: She once beat Jean Alberman at pinochle. She bragged about it for years. That's it.

(Pause.)

ALLEN: Why did you even have a funeral?

MARK: It's what she wanted.

(Fade to black. Lights rise again, on a podium. Allen stands and addresses the audience.)

ALLEN: *(In a rabbi cadence.)* We are-uh gathered here-uh today . . . to say a final farewell to Mrs. Sophie Sapstein, a . . . mother, a wife, a member of our community for her entire life . . . We see, today, in this room, her children, her grandchildren. *(Pause.)* Sophie Sapstein. I did not know Sophie Sapstein, it was my misfortune not to know her. And yet, I have heard of her . . . impact on our community. Her constancy. Her . . . consistency of purpose. She was the mother of Mark, Wallace, and Sarah. They are here. And the wife of Myron, who passed on some years ago, after many years of . . . marriage. She was an enthusiastic competitor. I understand she once won a game of pinochle with a friend, and that gave her much pride. *(Pause. He drops the rabbi cadence.)* I myself remember fondly the day when I beat my brother at Life. That was this board game, from Milton Bradley, the object was to get to the end of this track, which was life, it began with school, and then you got married — you were driving this little car, and when you got married you put this little pink peg in your car, next to your blue peg. And then more little pegs, when you had kids. Maximum of two. And then, you know, you picked a job, and made money, and had debts and at the end of the game if you had more money than debts you got to go to Millionaire Acres, and if you didn't, you went to the poorhouse. And that was it. And then, I thought: that's not right, there's one more space to get to, after this, and it's the same for everybody. But of course, the game designers probably thought, if everybody gets to the same exact place, what's the point of playing? Heh.

One of the terrible things about being a rabbi, frankly, is that people keep coming to us with their problems. Rabbi, I want to die; Rabbi, I'm going to die; Rabbi, my daughter is a drug addict, well, what am I supposed to do about it? I just read Hebrew and know how to talk funny. And you know, we get to the point where we look at you people all the same: you're all afflicted, you're all sick, it's fatal, you've only got a month to live, or fifty years, as the case may be. I'm sorry, I shouldn't have said anything about the daughter being a drug addict, that's really none of your business.

Sophie Sapstein. I did not know her. But I did know her, because there have been many like her. She confronted the natural order, which is that everything will come to nothing. She chose not to fool herself about this. She was in pain, so she inflicted pain on others. This is terrible. This is as common as fleas on a dog, in my opinion.

So do we mourn such a person? Why should we mourn such a person? Isn't the world better off? Maybe. But the world, to be perfectly frank, would probably be better off without all of us.

You, her family. Sophie Sapstein gave you life — you and you and you; and then through you, she gave it to your children. And that may be the worst thing she ever did. Because inherent in that gift was this moment: when you will lie insensate, vanished, forever, in a box, and someone who did not know you tries to avoid making anyone feel awkward.

We Jews, you know, we don't allow cremation. The supposed reason is, we're all going to need our bodies when the Messiah comes. But me, I think it's because the rabbis knew the value of a souvenir. We are, after all, a people who began by spending forty years schlepping a box through the desert . . . Sophie Sapstein will always be there, in this box, in plot forty-five west one eighteen of the Beth Shalom Jewish Cemetery off exit 22-A. You won't visit her, probably. But they will mow over her marker, so it can be seen, and she shall be there, in her silence, doing what the dead do. Which is to reproach us, for pretending that anything we do, any act of kindness or compassion, will prevent us from joining us them.

We all will end the game in the same space. And it is our defining absurdity to pretend that it matters how we get there. So let us say to Sophie Sapstein, a mean old lady who leaves no one sadder for her departure: you made it. You won. Congratulations to you, Sophie.

And you know what? All of us here. We will win, as well. We will try to do so more gracefully, more kindly, than Sophie did. But we will be here, someday, and we will want it said of us, as we say of Sophie, that we did not fail to rise up every day and act as if the smallest of things mattered tremendously. One way or another.

Now. Please rise for the Kaddish.

(Lights fade.)

END OF PLAY

THE BURIAL SOCIETY

by Susan Sandler

To Rose Eidels Sandler
"If I were drowned in the deepest sea . . ."

ORIGINAL PRODUCTION

The Burial Society premiered June 7, 2000, at HB Playwrights Theatre, New York; directed by Amy Saltz with the following cast:

Bella . . . . Dolores Sutton
Al . . . . Donald Buka

PLAYWRIGHT'S BIOGRAPHY

Susan Sandler's plays include *Crossing Delancey, The Burial Society, Hokey-Pokey, The Moaner, Kinfolks and Mountain Music, The Renovation, Tots,* and *My Tony,* which have been produced in New York at HB Playwrights, The Jewish Repertory Theatre, Ensemble Studio Theatre, All Seasons, and West Bank Café. Her plays have premièred regionally at Actors Theatre of Louisville, Capitol Rep, and she has had plays in repertory at regional theaters across the country. Ms. Sandler has written teleplays and screenplays for Warner Brothers, Sony Pictures, Twentieth Century Fox, Columbia, Polygram, Hallmark, CBS, Jersey Films, and Interscope, including *Crossing Delancey* and *Friends at Last.*

THE BURIAL SOCIETY

The waiting room of the Funeral Chapel just off the entrance to the chapel podium. Bella, blonde, is a well-maintained eighty. Al isa dapper man of indeterminate age.

BELLA: Do me.

AL: Not now.

BELLA: I'm begging you, do me, darling, do me.

AL: It's about to start.

BELLA: What do I care? I'm dying here.

AL: You can't wait 'til we get home?

BELLA: We'll never get home. This is gonna be an epic. They're starting with Meyer, poor soul, he forgets where he is, he goes into his "Yidl mit a fidel" we're here 'til next week.

AL: Everybody gets two minutes. That's the deal.

(Al opens the door to the chapel podium. We hear the speaker, Meyer, droning on . . .)

MEYER: *(Offstage. A fragile, hesitant voice.)* — The faces, the faces — oy, the faces, I look at you all, as far as my eyes will take me — who is here, who is gone, so many years we dream together — What does it add up? Hah? You give, you work, you love, and one day you look around and nobody is there — We are forgotten. The theater is empty, the lights are dark, and only you, my Yiddeleh, are left singing yourselves to sleep . . .

(Al closes the door.)

AL: Tops five minutes. They pull 'em off they go over five.

BELLA: Ha! — That'll be the day. You got Yiddish actors in front of a live audience, it's not a memorial service, its a matinee. — Come, do me.

AL: All right, all right.

(Al comes up behind Bella, removes her hat, she lets her head fall back against his stomach. He massages her temples gently.)

BELLA: Now she'll get her star in front of the Second Avenue Deli.

AL: Of course. What else.

BELLA: For what? A hanger-on. All her life she's playing minor characters — one national cottage cheese commercial — suddenly she's a diva.

AL: Shhhh — relax.

BELLA: What was she before she met Ben? — A *kur-veh,* a whore. He brought her to rehearsals in Warsaw, first she's making the tea, then she's handling the props, next thing, she's got a few lines. Believe me, before Ben she never was inside a theatre. In Poland she was garbage, plain and simple. *(She stands at the mirror, pulls her wig back in place. Adjusts the dramatic hairdo.)*

AL: It's history, Bella. Why are you scratching up dirt? — She's dead. She's not a threat to you. She's not gonna take your parts no more.

(Bella reels back — almost knocking Al over.)

BELLA: How dare you! Compare her to me? How dare you suggest she was ever my equal? — In *anything!*

AL: — Shah! I'm sorry, Bella — please — I never said that. I'm just saying show some respect. It's over.

BELLA: Take my parts — you said she took my parts. What parts?

AL: — I don't know.

BELLA: What parts?

AL: What does it matter? *Shane far farlen.* What's done is done.

BELLA: *What parts?*

AL: Personally, my opinion, you would have been a better "Rachel" in *The Golem.* One man's opinion, what do I know.

BELLA: I never wanted "Rachel" — "Gibron" is the role, I'm not a line counter, Al, you never seen me count lines. It's the complications, I love. The character has twists and turns, and a life inside bigger than the lines. This is what makes great acting and a great actor. Don't make me break my arm, patting myself, but Ben gave me the role because he knew only I, only Bella, could find the depth, the experience, the heartache to fulfill the character of "Gibron." The little prop girl wouldn't know where to begin.

AL: Yes, but a seamstress with whooping cough. And the character didn't even have a name, until you gave it to her.

BELLA: What are you *dreying* me with this garbage. You put my career next to her career — role by role, year by year, it's no contest. When she first joined the company, I swear to God, she would beg, *beg* to sit in and watch me rehearse. One night, I found her in my dressing room, polishing my boots — for *The Wedding Feast* —

AL: What? She was "Gertie," no?

BELLA: I'm telling you, she was polishing my boots! — She said, "I'm not worthy to be on the same stage with you, Bella, please let me do something to show my humility." So I let her polish. Meanwhile, she's asking me, "How would Gertie say this line? What should Gertie's reaction be here?" — And I'm giving her everything — line by line. That review she got in

The Forvitz, it should have read, "A heart-breaking performance by Hannah Zolefsky, but created by Bella Bellanka."

AL: She was a very good "Gertie." She made me cry. When her father throws her out of the house, I felt such emotions, this poor lost creature, torn between her love and her family — a black sin hanging over her like a curse from beyond —

BELLA: A curse — You wanna hear a curse? — She took the lines from me, Al — one by one she polished my boots, she listened, she learned, she sucked it from me — all I had to give. What she became, it was me. And how she repaid me, huh? *(Pause.)* How you *both* repaid me?

(Al whips around, his face gone white.)

AL: What? What are you talking?

BELLA: You think I don't know?

AL: What?

BELLA: You think I'm such a fool?

AL: What're you saying?

BELLA: The summer of '55, the mountains. You're playing "Fishbein the banker," she's the rebbitzen. And then I see, you're bringing her all the extra puddings every night at dinner. I'm watching and I'm thinking what's going on. Then I see you — in the trailer behind the handball court. Like animals. Once a whore, always a whore.

AL: *(Pleading, his voice going dry . . .)* Bella . . . Beelllla . . . it was centuries ago. *(Puts a hand on her shoulder, she pulls away.)* You know how it was — I had a certain — glamour, a following — they would line up after every performance — the girls, the women in the audience, they would stuff my pockets with perfumed letters, photographs, marriage proposals scribbled on the back of programs. It made me dizzy, what can I say?

BELLA: Everyone knew about you and Hannah. Everyone.

AL: No one knew. It was one time. I was weak, I was tempted. It was one time.

BELLA: You were more than tempted. You had your fill. It was every goddamn night, every time you could get away from me —

AL: Bella, look at me — look at me — Sixty-five years ain't bupkas, baby. It adds up. *(Pause.)* I made mistakes, but I always loved the right woman.

BELLA: We'll never know.

(Knock on the door.)

VOICE FROM THE NEXT ROOM: Bella — Meyer's finished — You're next.

(Bella moves to the door, stops at the mirror to adjust her hair, her scarf. She pulls herself up to her full height and moves slowly out to the podium beyond.)

(Al slumps into the chair.)

BELLA: *(At the microphone.)* When the history books record the last of the Yiddish Theatre, there will be many actors with glorious careers to remember, but one woman was held in the arms of her audiences with a special tenderness and a love that was like the love of a family for its favorite daughter, and I am speaking of Hannah Zolesfsky — an actress and a friend whose terrible loss we all feel today. She brought Yiddishkeit, Jewish heart, from her humble beginnings in Poland to her magnificent performances on the Yiddish stage, to the international stage of television where her famous words won America's hearts, "Hey, Frankie, if it's not Breakstone, it's not cottage cheese . . ."

END OF PLAY

CRIES FROM THE COCKPIT

by Tug Yourgrau

Original Production

Cries from the Cockpit was directed by Susan Einhorn with the following cast:

Jim . . . . Michael Countryman
Lorraine . . . . Claudia Fielding
Bobby . . . . David Troy
Eric . . . . Daniel Ahearn

Characters

JIM, mid-forties, a funeral director.
THE DECEASED, woman in her seventies.
LORRAINE, also mid-forties, a funeral director. Married to Jim.
BOBBY, around twenty. Intern.
ERIC, fifty-one. Jim's older brother. Embalmer.

Place

A funeral parlor. This is a top-of-the-line send-off. Downstage center, the coffin, a Balmoral by Casket Royale in dark hand-rubbed mahogany with peach-colored water silk EternaRest liner and solid brass handles (retail price $5,595) reposes on a draped stand. It is closed. A bounty of exotic flowers has been arranged tastefully about the room. Upstage stand two giant wreaths with sashes inscribed, "To the Best Grammy in the World" and "To Our Darling Mother, from All Her Children." Understated organ music plays over the PA.

Time

Early morning, the present.

CRIES FROM THE COCKPIT

Lights come up. After several seconds, the upstage door opens softly. Jim enters sipping coffee from a paper cup. He's in a dark suit. He inspects the setting with somber professionalism. He makes subtle adjustments to the flowers and wreaths. He crosses downstage to inspect the coffin. He strokes the dark wood. He takes out a handkerchief and polishes the brass hardware. Then, like a chef opening the oven to inspect a soufflé baked to perfection, he lifts the hinged lid on the top of the coffin. The coffin lid blocks the audience's view of the deceased.

JIM: Oh my God! *(He inspects the deceased.)* Jesus! *(He goes back to the door and shouts offstage.)* Lorraine!! LORRAINE!!

LORRAINE: *(Off.)* What?

JIM: COME HERE!

LORRAINE: *(Off.)* Stop shouting!

JIM: COME IN HERE RIGHT NOW!

(Lorriane enters, dressed in a formal dark suit.)

LORRAINE: Will you please quit shouting like that? They can hear you halfway round the block, for crying out loud!

JIM: Will you take a look at this, please?

LORRAINE: What? People are gonna start arriving in fifteen minutes, we don't have time for —

(Jim gestures to the deceased.)

LORRAINE: Oh, my God!

JIM: He must have put five quarts into her. And notice the nice touch on the mouth, just hanging open.

(He mimics how the deceased's mouth is hanging open.)

LORRAINE: Oh no! How did this happen?

JIM: That's what I want to know. Where the hell is Eric?

LORRAINE: I dunno, he must be at home.

JIM: Well, call him up and tell him to get his ass down here! Now!

LORRAINE: Oh, my goodness, they're gonna start showing up in — !

JIM: Call him!

(Lorraine exits. Jim opens the rest of the coffin.)

JIM: Goddamit!

(Lorraine comes back in with Bobby.)

JIM: Did you get a hold of Eric?

LORRAINE: No, just the machine. But Bobby here can fill us in.

BOBBY: I'm sorry, Mr. Ward. I am so sorry. I didn't know how to, it's not my fault!

JIM: Bobby?! Wait a minute! What the hell happened here?!

BOBBY: Does this mean I'm gonna get kicked out of the school?

LORRAINE: You're not gonna get kicked out of school. Just tell Mr. Ward what you told me.

(Bobby twists in uncertainty.)

BOBBY: Are you sure I'm not gonna get kicked out of — ?

JIM: Tell me, goddamit!

BOBBY: Eric asked me to . . . to finish up for him.

JIM: He *what?!!*

BOBBY: I knew you were gonna yell at me!

LORRAINE: Shouting won't help.

JIM: I'M NOT SHOUTING! *(Pause.)* I'm just . . . I'm sorry, Bobby. How do you mean, Eric asked you to finish her up?

BOBBY: He said he couldn't take it anymore. It was about one o'clock this morning and he'd been working on . . . on . . . on the face, I'm so sorry, Mr. Ward. I never in a million years would have — !

JIM: That's okay, Bobby, just tell me what happened.

BOBBY: Well, then he suddenly stopped and he said he couldn't keep going. He was crying. He said I should finish the embalming. He said it wasn't as hard as it looked.

JIM: Oh, fer chrissakes!

BOBBY: I told him I didn't know how to run the PortaBoy, I'd never — !

JIM: That does it! That . . . *idiot!* Him and his fucking . . . ! He's history!!

LORRAINE: Now, calm down, it doesn't help anything to just fly off the . . . you know he's very upset about —

JIM: We're all upset. That doesn't give him the right to . . . ! Hey, why are you making excuses for him?

LORRAINE: I'm not making excuses, I'm simply —

JIM: Yes, you are! You know you are! Why? Because he's so good at restorative, he's got the, the special *Hawaiian touch?!* He's such an . . . *artist,* we've all got to kowtow to him?

LORRAINE: Oh, Jim, really. Don't dig up all that stuff now, this isn't the time to — !

JIM: Because he's my *brother?!* Hey, nobody ever cut me any slack all these years, what gives him the right to get away with . . . ? HE'S HISTORY!

LORRAINE: This is hardly the time!! They'll be here in nine minutes, for God's sakes!

(Pause. Jim is thinking.)

BOBBY: I'm so sorry, Mr. Ward, I thought I'd turned the right —

JIM: It'll have to be a closed casket. We'll tell them something came up with —

LORRAINE: They're not gonna stand for that! They're all expecting an open casket, you know that!

JIM: Yeah? Well, things happen. *(Inventing.)* There was a bad chemical reaction.

LORRAINE: Oh, this is gonna end up costing us, this is gonna cost us in a big way!

(Pause.)

JIM: Goddam that Eric! Asking a first-year student to handle the most — !

BOBBY: I didn't know how to turn it off and I didn't want to splatter it all over the floor and I —

JIM: Bobby.

BOBBY: Please, Mr. Ward, don't report me to the, my grade point average is gonna — !

LORRAINE: I'm sure Mr. Ward is not going to report you to the —

JIM: Go down to the embalming room and fetch me up the PortaBoy, the number two trocar, and the stapler.

LORRAINE: Wait! Jim! What are you — ?!

JIM: And a bucket. A big one.

LORRAINE: No, for God's sakes, you're not gonna — !

JIM: Go, Bobby. Now! And come back right away!

BOBBY: Yessir, Mr. Ward.

(Bobby runs off.)

LORRAINE: You can't do that up here!

JIM: You got a better idea?

LORRAINE: But we could lose our license!

JIM: We're not gonna lose our license.

LORRAINE: Oh, yes, we will, what if someone . . . ? And you don't have enough time, my god, people are gonna start — !

JIM: You'll have to stall them when they get here.

LORRAINE: How am I gonna do that?

JIM: HOW THE HELL DO I KNOW?! Make something up! You're a funeral director!

LORRAINE: Did you take your pill this morning?

JIM: Yes, I took my pill!!

LORRAINE: Well, your blood pressure looks like it's gonna go through the —

JIM: Just keep 'em out till I'm done.

LORRAINE: Oh, this is ridiculous! You and that brother of yours are the most . . . !

(Lorraine leaves. Jim inspects the deceased's nostrils, removing and then reinserting the cotton balls. Bobby enters pushing a gleaming stainless steel cart with a large glass pump [the PortaBoy] connected to a long rubber tube with a two-foot-long, one-inch-thick stainless steel needle [the trocar] and another tube with a regular needle. There's also a large metal stapler shaped like a syringe.)

JIM: Bring it over here.

(Jim sheds his jacket as Bobby pushes the equipment in front of the coffin.)

JIM: Okay, get the needle into her arm.

(Bobby fumbles with the needle in her arm.)

JIM: No, no, not like that! You can't just bung it in anywhere! Jeez, no wonder she . . . Here, look. First you gotta find a vein, like this. Go ahead.

(Bobby tries again.)

JIM: There ya go. Now ease it in. . . . That's right. Now, gimme the trocar.

(Bobby hands him the trocar. Jim loosens the deceased's blouse and inspects the chest.)

JIM: What the . . . ? Jesus, Bobby, you didn't embalm the chest cavity?

BOBBY: I couldn't, Mr. Ward, I couldn't.

JIM: That's all right. Come here.

BOBBY: No, Mr. Ward!

JIM: Bobby. Come here . . . COME HERE!

(Bobby reluctantly comes over to him.)

JIM: Put your finger right here, below the sternum. Do it.

(Bobby reaches into the coffin.)

JIM: Good. Now, watch me carefully. You push in slowly. Slowly, like this.

(Jim inserts the trocar.)

BOBBY: Oh, Mr. Ward!

JIM: Stay with me, Bobby. *(Jim pushes harder.)* There. See? Now you're gonna get good penetration. Okay, turn it on.

(Bobby flicks on the PortaBoy, which begins to suck and wheeze. Yellow fluid drains from the hose into the bucket.)

JIM: Now that wasn't so bad, was it?

BOBBY: I don't know how you can do it, Mr. Ward. I don't think I could if it was —

(Lorraine sticks her head in.)

LORRAINE: Paul and Kim and the kids just arrived! They wanna come in and see her.

JIM: Well, they can't, goddamit, I'm not finished.

LORRAINE: How much longer?

JIM: I dunno, ten minutes.

LORRAINE: *Ten minutes?!* They won't stay out here that long, you can't expect —

JIM: Okay, then five minutes!

LORRAINE: Five. But really, just five.

(Lorraine closes the door.)

JIM: Keep your eye on the pressure. Don't let it get above fifteen pounds, or she'll blow up like a . . . *(Pause.)* Fucking temperamental . . . ARTIST! *(Jim grabs the stapler and starts firing staples into the deceased's gums, though the audience can't see it. The door opens.)* Lorraine, I said not . . .!

(Eric enters. He looks haggard.)

JIM: You! You prick! I oughtta . . .!

(Eric stares at the deceased.)

ERIC: I'll finish her mouth.

JIM: Get away! You're not touching her!

BOBBY: I'm so sorry, Eric. I didn't know how to use the trocar.

ERIC: I haven't slept at all. I've just been walking round and round. I don't know what to do, I don't —

JIM: Handing over a body to an untrained — ! You could have cost us our license, you son of a bitch! *(Jim keeps firing staples. Pause.)* I SAID GET OUT OF HERE!

ERIC: Jimmy. It took me six hours to finish the wax on her face. I wanted to get it just right. You know, how she'd get that little expression when she . . . ? I poured my heart into it. I had to start over three times, I was crying so hard.

BOBBY: You did a beautiful job.

ERIC: I couldn't drain her. Honest to God, Jimmy, I thought I could, but I couldn't. I just saw her lying there, and I felt so —

JIM: Your *job* is to prepare the body so that the family can get on with the grief work. That's your *job.* You said you'd do it, and you didn't do it. You left me holding the bag.

ERIC: Jimmy, don't be like this.

JIM: Get the hell out of here!

(Eric comes to the coffin and holds the deceased's hand. Jim keeps working.)

ERIC: I can't believe she's really —

JIM: She's *my* mother too, goddamit! SHE'S *MY* MOTHER TOO!

ERIC: But you've got Lorraine and the kids. I don't have anyone now. I'm all alone in the world.

JIM: Aw, gimme a break! Christ, that takes the cake! You are the most . . . ! Where the hell were you the two years she was practically a vegetable, huh? When Lorraine and I had to feed her and wash her down and wipe her ass? Did you ever think of her *then?* Or *us,* maybe we could have used a break?

ERIC: I couldn't see her like that. I just couldn't.

JIM: Oh God, no, of course not, not you, the "artist," the "sensitive one." You're out in Hawaii, you're a "restorative specialist." Lying on your ass on the beach feeling sorry for yourself is more like it.

ERIC: Jimmy, please, don't go on. For Mama's sake.

JIM: Too busy to come back and help out with your own mother. Until you ran out of money, that is. Then you knew where to come.

BOBBY: Mr. Ward, don't you think we'd better finish up Mrs. Ward so the people can — ?

ERIC: You hate me, I know you hate me.

JIM: And I send you money for I don't know how long, and I make excuses for you when Mom wants to know why her Eric won't come visit her when she's so sick and then I ask you to do this one thing, this *one little thing* for the family. After all these years. And you fuck it up!

ERIC: I loved her. I loved her so much.

(Eric tries to climb into the coffin. Lorraine sticks her head back in.)

LORRAINE: I can't hold 'em!

(Lights out.)

END OF PLAY

COPYRIGHT INFORMATION